D0879327

LEADING GOD'S PEOPLE

LEADING GOD'S PEOPLE

Wisdom from the Early Church for Today

Christopher A. Beeley

William B. Eerdmans Publishing Company

Grand Rapids, Michigan / Cambridge, U.K.

Published 2012 by

Wm. B. Eerdmans Publishing Co.

2140 Oak Industrial Drive N.E., Grand Rapids, Michigan 49505 /

P.O. Box 163, Cambridge CB3 9PU U.K.

Printed in the United States of America

17 16 15 14 13 12   7 6 5 4 3 2 1

Library of Congress Cataloging-in-Publication Data

Beeley, Christopher A.

Leading God's people: wisdom from the early church for today /

Christopher A. Beeley.

p.   cm.

Includes bibliographical references.

ISBN 978-0-8028-6700-1 (pbk.: alk. paper)

1. Christian leadership. 2. Pastoral theology. 3. Christian leadership —
History of doctrines — Early church, ca. 30-600. 4. Pastoral theology —
History of doctrines — Early church, ca. 30-600.   I. Title.

BV652.1.B39   2012

253 — dc23

2011039622

www.eerdmans.com

Contents

—◠◠—

[v]

Contents

Preface

When a surgeon performs a heart transplant, there is no question that an important work is being done. Family and friends hope that their loved one is receiving the best care available. For the patient it is a matter of life and death. Similarly, most people who need legal advice will try to find an attorney they can trust, someone with proven skill and competence. No one in their right mind wants to be represented by a lawyer who doesn't know what he or she is doing. And how many of us would entrust the management of our finances to someone who we know is a poor investor? Not many. In one example after another the value of professions that we consider truly important for our lives is obvious, and we naturally look for training, expertise, and wisdom in those we depend on.

The same holds true in the Christian Church. Most churchgoers know whether or not their leaders are providing effective ministry, to the point that many are even willing to change congregations in order to find the sort of pastoral leadership that truly feeds them. Clergy and lay leaders too have a sense of what faithful ministry looks like — at least we tend to recognize it when it is happening. Yet, regrettably, the opposite is the case far more often than we would like. Many Christians can remember a time when the church's leadership was less than inspiring, and church leaders (when we are honest with ourselves) know all too well when we are not practicing a ministry that is worthy of the calling to which we have responded.

When it is carried out faithfully and well, the leadership of the church is a truly wondrous thing. Effective pastoral ministry fosters a powerful experience of God's transforming presence in our lives and in the world around us. The benefits of faithful pastoral leadership are so great, in fact, that they touch every area of individual and social life. When we consider the nature of the Christian gospel, it is actually very strange that lapses in leadership occur at all, for time and again God provides immediate and abundant resources for the exercise of faithful ministry. The church has had many effective leaders throughout its history, people who were true to their calling and through whom God has inspired millions of believers to live courageous lives of faith, hope, and love. At the same time, pastoral ministry is a difficult and demanding work that requires great wisdom, skill, and commitment in order to practice well. Where, then, are church leaders to find God's help for the work that lies before them, and why do so many struggle as if they had been abandoned to their own devices? All over the globe churches in vastly different situations face a remarkably similar need for vital, strong leadership, now as much as ever before.

One of our greatest resources for effective ministry today comes from the period of the early church. Countless leaders over the centuries — Eastern and Western, Protestant, Catholic, and Orthodox — have found guidance and inspiration in the classic works on pastoral ministry written long ago. The purpose of this book is to present in a fresh and accessible way the key principles of church leadership as they were taught by some of the great theologians of the early church, all of whom were practicing pastors, whether bishops overseeing congregations or leaders of monastic communities. It is addressed primarily to clergy, lay leaders, seminarians, those exploring church leadership, and those responsible for the selection and supervision of church leaders: calling committees, regional and diocesan personnel, and bishops. For practicing church leaders it can serve to renew our understanding of ministry during a time of reflection, retreat, or regular weekly planning. For others, it offers a vision of the kind of leaders they hope to become.

The writing of this book has taken place in the company of many others. It took shape through my teaching at Yale Divinity School and Berkeley Divinity School at Yale, and at clergy conferences and church leadership meetings in the United States and the United Kingdom. Without fail, whenever I have discussed the principles of pastoral leadership from the early church with colleagues in ministry, I have been reminded just how vital they still are for the church's life today. As little as a hundred years ago, clergy in most denominations would have read some of the classic works on pastoral ministry by Augustine, John Chrysostom, or Gregory the Great, but today they have fallen out of the curricula of most seminaries and divinity schools. This book aims to make newly available the great depth and richness of early Christian reflection on church leadership in order to strengthen the church in all of its contemporary forms.

First, a brief word about the authors and works themselves. The sources of early Christian pastoral theology are scattered and quite varied. They begin with a few, short passages in the New Testament, such as 1 Timothy 3 and 1 Peter 5, followed by sporadic comments in homilies, commentaries, letters, theological treatises, and church orders written between the second and the fourth centuries. Beginning in the fourth century, theologians wrote the first full-scale descriptions of pastoral ministry, synthesizing much of what came before while continuing to base themselves on the scriptures above all. Ever since that time, these works have remained the most helpful and enduring guides for church leadership that we possess, second only to the Bible. They have been useful in a variety of Christian communities, church styles, and denominational structures, and they remain among our greatest resources for the practice of church leadership.

St. Gregory of Nazianzus, also known as Gregory the Theologian (c. 329-390), was one of the three "Cappadocian Fathers" and later became one of the three "Universal Teachers" of Eastern Orthodoxy. He served as bishop of Constantinople and president of the Council of Constantinople in 381, which produced the "Nicene Creed" of today's eucharistic liturgies. Gregory wrote the first extant treatise on pastoral ministry in Christian tradition, his oration *On the Priesthood.* St. Ambrose (c. 339-397) was bishop of Milan, the capital of the Western Roman Empire, a renowned preacher and biblical interpreter, and one of the instrumental causes of the conversion of St. Augustine. Ambrose wrote several works on the practice of ministry, the most important being *The Duties of Leaders.* Augustine (354-430) was the bishop of Hippo in North Africa and the leading theologian of his generation. Augustine's teaching on countless subjects was so brilliant that he eventually became the chief architect of Western Christendom. His main work on church leadership is *Christian Teaching,* which concentrates on biblical interpretation and preaching; also important are many passages in his sermons and letters. Originally a monk, St. John Chrysostom (c. 347-407) served as patriarch of Constantinople until he was ousted by his political and ecclesiastical enemies. John's famous work *On the Priesthood* drew heavily on Gregory Nazianzen and later came to be read throughout the Eastern and the Western churches. St. John Cassian (c. 365-433), also a monk, was a great synthesizer of previous monastic traditions in Egypt, Palestine, and Italy. His remarks on pastoral ministry in his *Conferences* and *Institutes* were a major influence on the *Rule of Benedict,* which itself formed the basis of most later Western monastic orders. Finally, Pope Gregory I (c. 540-604), or Gregory the Great, was one of the most outstanding occupants of the see of Rome in the first millennium. Gregory's *Pastoral Rule,* which is based primarily on Gregory Nazianzen and Augustine, became the chief manual on church leadership, and a work of wider social and political importance, in the Eastern and Western Middle Ages. Current editions of each work are listed at the end of the book, for those who want to study early pastoral theology in greater depth.

The benefits of effective church leadership are hardly limited to the Christian faithful alone. It is my deep conviction that the vitality of the church holds enormous potential for the well-being of the many societies in which we live. It is to this wider end, and above all to the glory of God, that this book is offered.

I

The Leadership of the Church

—ɷ—

Keep watch over yourselves and over the flock, of which the Holy Spirit has made you overseers, to shepherd the Church of God that he has obtained with the blood of his own Son.

Acts 20:28

Anyone who has attended Sunday services knows how crucial church leadership is. When strong leadership is present, we appreciate it palpably, and the entire community benefits in tangible ways. When it is lacking, we know that something of central importance is missing, and we rightly lament its absence. In every period of history Christians have had cause to reflect on what may seem an obvious fact: the effectiveness of the church's leadership is crucial to its vitality and faithfulness, its spiritual health, and its fulfillment of God's mission in the world.

Scripture, tradition, and the experience of countless believers show that God has designed the church in such a way that someone needs to be in charge of each Christian community. Particular people — most often a senior pastor together with assistant clergy and laypeople — are officially entrusted with the authority of leadership for the sake of the entire body. But this is not an automatic thing, as if having appointed leaders were enough in itself. The *way* in which leadership is exercised is of the utmost importance for the church's life and well-being. While we may regret those instances in which solid leadership was absent or severely impaired, we can also be grateful that there have been so many outstanding church leaders throughout history, beginning with the apostles themselves. Since the first generation of the church there have been distinct leaders, and the basic character and rationale of this leadership is surprisingly well-defined across a variety of cultural, geographical, and historical differences.

The Origins and Importance of Church Leadership

Before we look at the basic identity and work of church leaders, it may be helpful to consider the earliest beginnings of leadership office. The New Testament gives little explicit description of the roles and functions of church leaders, just as it also lacks a formal order of worship. Yet the apostolic writings clearly indicate that leadership was both necessary and centrally important. Jesus himself appointed a distinct group of twelve disciples, with an inner circle of three (Peter, James, and John) and a predominant leader among them (Peter). The gospels record that Jesus spent most of his time and attention with these twelve, and it was to them that he entrusted the furtherance of his mission after his death, resurrection, and ascension. The apostles, who soon included Paul and others, carried on the authority and the work of leadership, including the spread of the gospel and the planting of new churches among peoples and territories beyond

Palestine and the Jewish Diaspora. As a result of this spread, it eventually became necessary to appoint new local leaders in each community. In the Pastoral Epistles (1-2 Timothy and Titus) — so named in the modern period because they give unprecedented attention to the office and duties of pastoral leadership[1] — we see the further stabilization of distinct leadership offices in second- or third-generation communities.[2] In recognition of Paul's apostolic authority, many later writers looked to him as the premier example of pastoral or episcopal leadership.

In the New Testament church leaders are commonly, though not exclusively, referred to as overseers or bishops *(episkopoi)* as well as elders or presbyters *(presbyteroi)*.[3] These two terms are often used interchangeably; and while there may have been a distinct supervisor (bishop) among the group of overseer-elders, they are not clearly demarcated as a radically distinct office. In addition to these primary leaders, all of whom are considered servants or ministers *(diakonoi)*, we occasionally find another group called "deacons" in a more particular sense (also *diakonoi*). It appears that by the time of the Pastoral Epistles, these functions developed into three distinct offices which were either instituted or supported by the laying on of hands. Yet even here we have relatively little indication of the degree of formality or of all the functions associated with each office.

The simplest and most telling description of early pastoral leadership comes in Paul's address to the leaders from Ephesus in the Acts of the Apostles. According to Luke the evangelist (who wrote Acts), Paul tells the Ephesian elders *(presbyteroi)* that the Holy Spirit has appointed them to be overseers *(episkopoi)* as shepherds of God's church (Acts 20:28). Paul calls the same group both presbyters and bishops; he regards their authority as having come from the Holy Spirit; and he characterizes their ministry as that of pastoring, or shepherding sheep. Also illuminating is the following statement in 1 Peter:

> I exhort the elders *(presbyteroi)* among you to tend the flock of God that is in your charge, exercising the oversight *(episkopountes)*, not under compulsion but willingly, as God would have you do it — not for sordid gain but eagerly. Do not lord it over those in your charge, but be examples to the flock. And when the chief shepherd appears, you will win the crown of glory that never fades away. (1 Pet. 5:1-4)

In both passages the apostles instruct the presbyter-bishops to act as overseers and shepherds of God's sheep in such a way that they will earn the approval of Christ, who is the Great Shepherd.

During the first generation of the church particular apostles exercised supervisory authority over the communities in their charge, such as James in Jerusalem and Paul among his Gentile and Jewish-Gentile churches (we know less about Peter's later ministry). There is also evidence of a single person who acted as a chief leader among the group of local presbyter-bishops, a practice that eventually produced the distinct supervisory office of bishop. By the time the apostles receded into the background, we find more frequent references to a single bishop — possibly in the Pastoral Epistles and certainly in the letters of Bishop Ignatius of Antioch, which date from the early-second century (roughly contemporaneous with the Pastorals), and in most writers afterward. The development of a singular supervisory office is notoriously murky, yet it is in keeping with the initial apostolic pattern, and it became the norm in most churches by the end of the second century, as it still is today.[4]

Despite the great importance of these earliest witnesses,

they are rare and relatively brief. It is only from later generations that we have any extensive treatment of church leadership. One of the most striking things about these later works
is the extent to which they agree on basic principles, particularly if we consider the great diversity of early Christian communities. For example, each of the early sources speaks of the
crucial importance of pastoral leadership for the life of the
community. Gregory of Nazianzus echoes earlier writers by
placing a special emphasis on the role that pastoral leaders
play. God has providentially arranged the church so that certain people are distinctly gifted, called, and ordained to serve
as leaders for the sake of the rest of the community, just as the
different organs in the human body work to preserve its
overall health and vitality.[5] Bishops and priests serve as "leaders of men and women" in the most basic matters of the
Christian life, and they preside over the community gathered
in worship.[6] Similarly, in a letter to a church that was about to
elect a new bishop, Gregory of Nyssa defines a bishop as "a
leader, a superior, a teacher of piety, and a director of the hidden mysteries," that is, the Eucharist.[7]

In one of his sermons, Augustine speaks movingly of
God's provision of pastoral leadership for the church:

> It is unthinkable that good shepherds could be lacking
> now. Far be it from us that they should be lacking — far
> be it from God's mercy not to produce them and estab-
> lish them! Of course, if there are good sheep, there are
> also good shepherds, because good shepherds are made
> out of good sheep.[8]

The provision of leadership is fundamental for the life of the
church; it is unthinkable that the one would exist without the
other. In another sermon, on Psalm 127, Augustine gives an
exquisite description of pastoral authority: "Jerusalem has its

vigilant guardians. Just as it has its builders, the workers who labor on the building, so too does it have its watchmen (see Psalms 126/127:1)." He observes how vigilantly the Apostle Paul guarded a church in his charge:

> He was guarding it, he was its keeper, he kept watch to the utmost of his ability over those committed to his care. And this is what bishops do still. A higher position is assigned to them precisely so that they can oversee the people and guard them. . . . In a vineyard a watchtower is provided for the worker responsible for the vineyard's safety, so that he or she can keep an eye on it; and similarly a higher station is accorded to bishops.[9]

Each of the great pastoral theologians of the early church not only regard leadership as divinely instituted; they also consider the quality of that leadership essential to the church's vitality, faithfulness, and effectiveness in carrying out God's mission.

In this book we will be focusing on the primary leaders of the church — its bishops, priests, or pastors. Yet, as we have already seen, pastoral leadership is often shared among a team of various ministers, and most of the elements of pastoral ministry are exercised by the laity as well. Our discussion of primary church leadership therefore applies to many types of service. There are several different terms used for church leaders in early Christian sources, much as there are among today's churches. Yet the most common single term, and the one that most aptly describes the nature and work of church leadership as a whole, is "pastor" or "shepherd." Above all else, church leaders are those who shepherd God's flock on behalf of Christ, the Great Shepherd. We will therefore speak throughout the book about the ministry of pastoral leadership, knowing that much of what we discuss applies to the priesthood of all believers.

The early sources typically refer their thoughts on pastoral ministry to "bishops," a term that also needs some explanation. For many centuries bishops functioned primarily as senior pastors of particular Christian communities, even after they began to exercise wider authority over other clergy in a given region. Not only did bishops remain practicing local pastors, but the other functions they performed were based on their spiritual authority within their own communities. This applies to famous metropolitan bishops such as Basil of Caesarea and Augustine of Hippo, who regularly ministered as pastors to their congregations. In the early church a "bishop" was first and foremost a pastor, not an administrative official. When we speak here of bishops, we are therefore talking about the primary leaders of local churches, and we are reminded that all types of church leadership are rooted in pastoral ministry.

It is also important to note that patristic theologians, like the New Testament documents, give essentially the same advice to presbyters or priests that they do to bishops.[10] The reason is that their ministries are seen to be essentially the same, even though bishops have the extra responsibility of supervision. I will therefore speak interchangeably of pastors, bishops, priests, and presbyters in the pages that follow. If the language of "bishops" and "priests" is familiar to readers in more catholic traditions, then the language of the "pastorate" and "presbyterate" will serve to remind them of the chief functions of such leaders. And if readers in Reformed traditions are more used to the terms "pastor" and "elder" (or "presbyter"), then they can appreciate that the language of "bishop" and "priest" has been the accepted terminology for millions of Christians throughout history and is also not without biblical precedent.

Service with Authority

It is common to think of pastoral ministry as a kind of service, and so it is. But before we consider its servant-like quality, it is important to appreciate the real power that leaders carry in their communities and in the lives of individual people. Like actual shepherds, Christian pastors exercise a clear and necessary authority over their flocks, by which they are able to guide the members of the church toward God. In the earliest document in the New Testament, Paul speaks of the authority of leadership in very strong terms. He admonishes the church in Thessaloniki to have respect for "those who labor among you and have charge over you in the Lord and admonish you." Because of their work, leaders are to be "highly esteemed in love" (1 Thess. 5:12-13). Similarly, we see Jesus giving the twelve disciples great "power and authority" to cast out demons, heal diseases, and preach the gospel (Luke 9:1).[11] Such authority has been fundamental to church leadership since its earliest beginnings, and in every age the church has needed strong and authoritative pastors.

People naturally look to their pastors for competent leadership, and they expect them to hold real authority, otherwise they would look elsewhere or simply help themselves. An effective pastoral relationship depends entirely on the authority that leaders receive from Christ through the Holy Spirit and on the accompanying set of projections and expectations that church members ascribe to them. In the early second century Ignatius of Antioch wrote to the church in Ephesus that, in order to be sanctified by God, they must submit to the teaching and the sacramental authority of the bishop and presbytery.[12] Gregory Nazianzen too emphasizes that priestly ministry is a form of command that carries real authority, responsibility, and the power of spiritual governance, even as it is also a form of service carried out in great humility. Without this authority, he adds, the health of the entire community suffers greatly.[13]

Who would want to consult a doctor or a lawyer who lacks the ability and expertise necessary to do the job? It is the same in the church: Christians, and even many unbelievers, rightly expect pastoral leaders to know what they are doing and to be able to do it. On the authority of the pastorate John Chrysostom writes,

> God has given to priests a power greater than that of our natural parents. The two are as different as the present and the future life, for our natural parents bring us into this life, but priests bring us into the life to come. . . . They have often saved a sick soul, or one that was on the point of perishing.[14]

People sometimes have mixed feelings about whether to expect the same excellence from church leaders that they do from other professions. Some believe that the church should not be so exacting in its standards, whether out of a misguided sense of compassion or a fear of authority. At the opposite extreme, others have an inflated sense of what pastoral authority involves, believing that leaders can practically do their people's religion for them.

The apostles and the early theologians urge us to be very clear about the power that pastoral leaders carry. Simply put, church leaders are capable of doing either enormous good or great harm. In order to promote constructive leadership and to avoid the potential dangers that exist, it is imperative to understand the true nature of pastoral authority, for what we do not understand we are more likely to abuse. Competent, helpful, and safe Christian leaders are confident in the purpose and the influence of their work, and they are deeply humbled by the privilege of serving God and others in this way.

Speaking of pastoral authority can raise concerns about the ways in which certain leaders have abused their authority and harmed those in their charge. This is a serious problem, and one that the early sources addressed with great earnestness, as we will see in the next chapter. For now, we must remind ourselves that such abuses do not undermine the validity of strong and authoritative leadership any more than a bad doctor makes the work of good doctors less necessary. If anything, the regrettable abuses of the pastoral office further highlight the qualities of good leadership, and they show us how important it is that leaders understand and remain faithful to the true nature of their authority.

The authority that pastoral leaders carry is none other than the power of God. The power that creates the universe and calls new life into being is the very same power that manifests itself in the humility that led Jesus to offer his life for our salvation. In order to be helpful and constructive leaders, Christian pastors must exercise a divine authority that is very different from the abusive power of the world. True church leaders are never authoritar*ian,* but they expresses the power that is proper to God, as Jesus makes clear in a famous gospel passage. When James, John, and the other disciples began to quarrel about receiving honor and glory for themselves on the basis of their special roles in Jesus' mission, Jesus rebuked them by contrasting his own authority with that of the world: "Whoever wants to be great among you must be your servant, . . . for the Son of Man came not to be served but to serve, and to give his life as a ransom for many" (Mark 10:42-45). It is in this sense that pastoral authority is always that of a servant, while at the same time being a very real potency that is capable of overcoming sin and death.

The main point of pastoral authority is to serve the church as a shepherd in the manner of Jesus, drawing on the resources that God has given us in order to be of benefit to others, rather than asserting our own prerogative. Augustine states it poignantly: "We [bishops] have been set before you, yet we are servants; we 'preside' — but only if we are 'profitable'!"[15] Servant leadership does not mean a lack of confidence, purpose, or strength — quite the contrary. It means that leaders make it their chief aim to love God and to promote the spiritual well-being of others. In a sermon for the ordination of a fellow bishop, Augustine stresses this central character of pastoral leadership:

> The one who presides over the people ought to understand before he begins that he is the servant of many. And let him not disdain this role; I repeat, let him not disdain to be the servant of many, because the Lord of lords did not disdain to serve us. . . . And the advice and warning I'm giving, I am also afraid of myself![16]

Gregory the Great reiterated Augustine's point in one of his most memorable sayings: bishops are the "servants of the servants of God."

There are two main types of confusion about pastoral authority. The first is that there is no such thing. This view amounts to saying that the church is best served by weak leaders who are ignorant and incapable of doing their job. In recent decades, for example, some have suggested that in order to promote the ministry of all the baptized and to strengthen the people of God, ordained leaders need to get out of the way, or relinquish their duties — the implication being that strong laity require weak or absent clergy. But such an idea runs entirely counter to the teaching of Jesus, the apostles, and the leaders of the early church, and it is debilitating to the church. Weak leadership does not promote vital lay ministry; it compromises the health of the entire body by failing to provide the laity with the basic spiritual guidance they need in order to be effective leaders themselves.

The second type of confusion is the belief that pastoral authority is about bossing people around and seeking one's own honor and prestige. This problem is equally destructive, and it is obviously forbidden by Christ himself. Gregory the Great echoes Jesus' warning in strong terms: "Whoever turns the ministry of pastoral leadership into an opportunity for domination is justly numbered among the hypocrites."[17] Pastoral authority is never meant to inflate the egos of leaders at the expense of those they lead. A pastor must never push people around to serve his or her own personal gain, either by actively bullying them or by manipulating them in more passive ways. Such treatment is very far from the power of Jesus Christ, and in fact it betrays an underlying *lack* of strength, and an absence of real authority.

To avoid both errors, we should imagine pastoral leadership as both servant-like authority and authoritative service. This means that church leaders exercise their authority not by throwing their weight around, but by helping to build others up. And they serve others not by pretending they have nothing to offer, but by being real spiritual guides. Both of these tasks are very hard work and require great strength and deep humility. In another sermon, Augustine explains: "You see, the one who gives useful orders is serving you, serving you by watching over you, serving you by taking care of you, serving you by worrying over you — serving you, finally, by loving you." And the greatest form of love, he continues, is to lay down one's life for one's friends, just as Jesus did.[18] Church leaders, in other words, must lead in such a way as to promote the well-being of their people, and they serve their people by being effective leaders in Christ. There are many ways in which people need help and assistance, and it is a noble work to provide for them all; but not all forms of service are pastoral ministry. In order to be faithful and helpful leaders, pastors must maintain their focus on serving people specifically as shepherds and guides in the Christian life. This is a paradox that lies at the very heart of the gospel and one that we see embodied in Christ himself. Only the all-powerful Son of God, the co-creator of the universe, could save us from sin and death by humbling himself and dying on the Cross; and only the one who was willing to love his friends to the point of death could make available the saving power that he possessed by nature from eternity. In the kingdom of God authority and service, power and humility are two sides of the same coin.

The wisdom of the early saints shows that the work of pastoral ministry is both exceedingly important and extremely demanding. For this reason it is indeed a high office and a noble calling, and it requires the sort of power and strength that can only come from God. The church needs strong and capable shepherds to guide it toward its eternal life with Christ. The more clergy and laity expect, support, and rejoice in strong, life-giving leadership, the more effective will be the ministry of the church as a whole.

All for Others

In speaking of church leadership as ministry and service, we come to one of its most difficult challenges. What makes pastoral leadership a form of service is not that it is weak or ineffective, as we have just observed, but that it is focused on God and others, not on the leaders themselves. At the end of the day and at the end of a lifetime of ministry, the only thing that matters is whether we have made the love of God and the spiritual growth of our people the top priority. What most excites a true pastor is not his or her reputation or advancement, but the growth and well-being of the church.

The most explicit statement of this point in the New Testament comes in Paul's letter to the Ephesians: Christ gives us gifts for ministry "to equip the saints for the work of ministry, for building up the body of Christ, until all of us come to the unity of the faith and of the knowledge of the Son of God, to maturity, to the measure of the full stature of Christ" (Eph. 4:12-13). Jesus gives the same emphasis in his charge to Peter at the end of John's gospel. When Peter tells Jesus that he loves him, Jesus tells Peter simply, "Feed my sheep," and to follow him through the trials to come (John 21:15-19). Similar statements appear throughout the works of the church fathers. Gregory Nazianzen writes that the entire purpose of leadership is to promote the good of the whole body.[19] Augustine delivered a sermon on the anniversary of his own ordination in which he spoke directly about the focus of his ministry: "This burden of mine, about which I am now speaking — what else is it, after all, but *you?*" He then went on to pray that Jesus would help him to carry that burden.[20] Great church leaders in every age have reminded us that our primary duty and the greatest source of our joy as leaders is to see our people grow in Christ.

The focus of pastoral leadership is so consistently on the people, in fact, that the spiritual condition of the flock is the only real measure of a leader's success. Paul invokes the same idea when he defends his apostolate to those in Corinth who were contesting it. Significantly, he does not point to his own credentials or try to give evidence of his abilities. Instead he says that his letter of recommendation is the Corinthians themselves, "a letter of Christ prepared by us, written not with ink but with the Spirit of the living God, not on tablets of stone but on tablets of human hearts" (2 Cor. 3:1-3). Similarly, Ambrose comments that leaders of real distinction are those who "win their victories in the contests that their disciples undergo, rather than in their own."[21] Although the world and our own vanity would have us think otherwise, the reputation of pastors is won by the fruitful lives of those they serve. So Ambrose admonishes all church leaders: "Show your virtue in your spiritual children."[22] When pastors make it their sole aim to build up the church, then the reverse is true as well, that the praise of a teacher brings honor to the church as a whole.[23] But unless we are truly devoted to the good of our flocks, such praise will be dangerous flattery.

We will further consider the quality of pastoral humility in the next chapter. For now we must simply note that the sole object of effective church leadership is God and the well-being of the church. Of course this all sounds obvious as soon as we say it — church leaders are supposed to build up the church, are they not? But if we are honest with ourselves, we know that it is much easier said than done. For both clergy and laity to stay focused on the growth of the church is a real challenge, and there would not be so many admonitions to do so in the tradition if it were not. It is very difficult for clergy to conquer their vainglory and keep their focus solely on Christ and the good of his flock, just as it is difficult for laity to avoid escaping the difficulties of their lives and the needs of the world through their adulation of the clergy. Yet whenever we make anything other than the glory of God and the up-building of his church our chief purpose, we have abandoned our calling and are derelict in our duty.

Augustine asks sharply,

> What kind of bishop is called one, but isn't one really? The one who enjoys his status more than the welfare and salvation of God's flock — who at this pinnacle of ministry "seeks his own advantage, not that of Jesus Christ" (Phil. 2:21). He is called a bishop, but he isn't a bishop. It's an empty name. . . . "Whoever desires the office of bishop, is setting his heart on a good work" (1 Tim. 3:1)

— yes! But desiring the office of bishop isn't desiring the office of bishop in itself; it is "setting your heart on a good work."

Augustine is reminding us that the only thing that matters about being a bishop, priest, or pastor is the work of service that we undertake for the flock of Christ. If we desire anything other than this — particularly our own advantage — we have falsified the office of leadership, and it is not really the pastoral office we seek. Augustine comes straight to the point:

> "I want to be a bishop; oh, if only I were a bishop," someone says. Would that you were! Are you seeking the name, or the real thing? . . . Yes, I will be so bold as to say that there are no bad bishops, because if they are bad, they aren't bishops![24]

Here we are being invited to see the difference between reality, which is to say God's point of view, and the worldly pretensions with which people can (for a time) fake something as sacred as church leadership. In reality Christians live as citizens of God's kingdom, and we profess our allegiance to God's truth, which will, in the final Day of the Lord, become fully manifest and reveal everything that has been hidden or distorted. In reality there is no such thing as a church leader who uses the office for his or her own advantage instead of building up the body of Christ. Such people are only pretending to be pastors or bishops, and their pretense will one day be revealed for what it is. The apostles and the early saints continually warn the leaders of the church that we must very wary of wanting to hear ourselves called shepherds more than we want to do the *work* of a shepherd; and this applies just as well to lay leaders as it does to clergy.[25]

It is especially crucial that we appreciate the point when

ordination processes tend to become overly inward and subjective. The traditional warnings against self-concern are not designed merely to regulate the psychology of pastoral leaders — as if, again, we were the main focus. Rather, they are a reflection of what the church is. The focus of pastoral leadership is on the people because all Christians, not church leaders as such, are the primary ministers of the gospel. It is the church as a whole that is God's "chosen race, royal priesthood, and holy nation" (2 Pet. 2:9). Pastoral leaders serve to build up the body of Christ, so that the entire church can bring the gospel of Jesus Christ to a very broken world. Augustine asks his congregation, "Do you think only we who stand up here proclaim Christ and you yourselves do not? . . . It is the whole church that preaches Christ."[26] Oftentimes the laity need to be reminded of this as much as clergy. In another sermon Augustine cautions his flock against inflating his pride as their leader: "Whatever we [clergy] may be, don't let your hope rest on us. . . . I want to rejoice over you, not to be puffed up by you!"[27] The apostles and the great church leaders of every age are absolutely united on this point: the office of church leadership exists solely for the sake of the flock, never for the glory and prestige of its occupants. To be sure, pastoral ministry should be a satisfying and joyful work, but it will be so only if our focus remains on the good of our flock, which is our true delight as leaders.

In this sense church leadership is very much like the Christian life itself, where only by losing our lives through the love of Christ and our neighbor do we truly find them. The satisfaction, joy, and high esteem that leaders experience are always bound up in the good of those they serve. When it is done well, which is to say when our focus remains on God and the good of our flock, then pastoral ministry is an excellent example of what recent leadership theorists have called a "win-win" situation. The stronger and more faithful the pastor, the stronger and more faithful the community will be, and vice versa, just as by seeking God's kingdom first will we come to have everything else besides (Matt. 6:33). But the reverse of this principle is extremely insidious, and it is destructive of the church's life. It can be easy to fall into the trap of assuming that the success and well-being of both leaders and people inevitably conflict with one another — that the church is, in short, a zero-sum game, where one person's good or voice or authority can only exist at the expense of another's. This sort of thinking has sabotaged innumerable ministry initiatives, and it lies behind any effort to promote the ministry of either clergy or laity that depends on diminishing the strength and presence of the other. This can occur when clergy believe they should boss people around rather than help them to discover their own gifts for ministry, or when clergy are replaced with laity in liturgical and other official functions. The former approach diminishes the laity in an obvious way, but the latter undermines lay ministry as well because it reinforces the insulting view that only clergy, or laity who have become quasi-clergy, are real Christians. Whenever any of us (clergy or laity) forgets that the full body of Christ and its ministry in the world are the real object of our concern, we are no longer thinking about the kingdom of God, but instead about the kingdom of the world. Strong and effective pastoral leadership cannot possibly conflict with the vitality and the ministry of the laity, because it is for the sake of all the baptized that it exists at all! The sooner we abolish all thoughts to the contrary, the better off the church will be.

The importance of community-focused leadership holds important implications for the selection and training of future leaders. The qualities, abilities, and commitments needed for church leadership are of course deeply personal; above all, they include the candidate's knowledge of God and experience of the grace of Christ. But if pastoral leadership is aimed at the benefit of the whole church, then such qualities will ultimately be discerned by the community even more than by the individual candidate. Throughout the early church the selection of new leaders was profoundly social. Most bishops were chosen by the election, or at least the approval, of the local community,[28] and they often came from within the community to begin with, having risen through the ranks of various ministerial offices. There are many examples of notable leaders — people such as Gregory Nazianzen, Ambrose, and Augustine — who never even wanted to become bishops but were called upon to do so by their communities, because the people or some other leader recognized in them true gifts for pastoral ministry.

Since pastoral ministry is oriented toward the well-being of the community, the qualities and gifts that are necessary for good leadership are, by definition, ones that are most reliably perceived by others. If we look at it from the community's point of view, it should be obvious that, in the long run, people are the best judges of whether or not they are being fed. From the perspective of the individual candidate, it is equally important to recognize how easily we can deceive ourselves, and how much better other people sometimes know us than we do ourselves. The record of the saints shows that, until we have been shaped, trained, and appointed to our respective ministries, our inward sense of calling can be either true or false when we are left to our own devices. In many of today's ordination processes, far too much emphasis is placed on the candidate's inward sense of vocation, which reflects an unhealthy kind of subjectivism. In the selection process and throughout a lifetime of ministry, the perceptions and faith-experience of the community should be the greatest indicator of leadership potential and success. In the individual candidate, the surest sign of a pastoral vocation is a recognizable desire to build up the church, with some awareness of its joy and satisfaction as well as its labor and difficulty. Any other form of personal self-fulfillment is misleading in the selection process, and it will cause even greater problems down the road, when pride and vainglory become enormous impediments to the exercise of a faithful ministry.

For all these reasons, the candidate's inward sense of calling is much less important compared to the discernment of the community. One can enter pastoral leadership either by willingly seeking it, or by being urged to do so by others; it makes little difference where we begin. As Gregory Nazianzen observes, there have been certain people who did want to be leaders, such as Aaron and Isaiah, but there were others who positively dreaded the prospect of leadership, such as Moses and Jeremiah. Whether one flees the pastoral office out of a healthy fear of its difficulties, a desire for quieter occupation, or a humble sense of unworthiness, such reluctance is just as laudable as the straightforward desire of those who, out of love of the church and obedience to God's call, embrace it wholeheartedly.[29] It is perfectly fine if one aspires to be a pastor or bishop, as 1 Timothy 3:1 says, but it is not strictly necessary. In either case, the community's discernment of the prerequisite qualities is the chief criterion, because what matters above all, from initial selection through a lifetime of ministry, is the growth of the church in Christ.

In Christ

The sort of leadership that is focused on building up the church is the clearest representation of Christ, who is the primary Shepherd of his church. Just as pastoral leaders empower the ministry of all the baptized, so too they share in the ministry of Christ himself. Here again it is tempting to imagine a conflict where there is none: if some worry that strong leaders get in the way of the laity, others may fear that they get in the way of Christ. Nothing could be farther from the truth. According to the scriptures and early Christian tradition, strong and faithful pastors are the best representation of Christ's shepherding, not obstacles that stand in Christ's way. The more effectively church leaders do their work, the more the church will experience the ministry of Christ in their midst. For just as Christ has empowered all believers to participate in his own life and calling, so too has he empowered the leaders of the church to share in his own work of pastoral ministry. Christ is most present to his people as their Shepherd when the church is being led by competent pastors who are clear about the nature of their work and are dedicated to it wholeheartedly.

It may be easiest to understand the point from the other side, by considering what it looks like when church leaders do oppose Christ. Simply put, human shepherds conflict with Christ's shepherding when they are unfaithful and ineffective. It is only bad shepherds, in other words, who oppose Christ, not good ones. In a real, mystical sense, Christ *is* the only Shepherd of the church when it is being well led by its human pastors, because they can be good shepherds only by remaining "in Christ," as Jesus and Paul so frequently say of the Christian life in general.[30] Amma Sarah reminds us that all of our works in the Christian life, however much we may exert ourselves, are at a deeper level the works of Christ our Lord.[31] To be a good pastor means precisely to be in Christ, just as it is the mark of an unfaithful shepherd to be separated from Christ. Conflict between church leaders and Christ is therefore a mark of *un*faithfulness, not the result of true leadership.

Augustine reflects insightfully on the unity of good bishops with Christ, and the separation of bad bishops from him:

All good shepherds are in the one Shepherd; they are one. They feed the sheep, and Christ feeds them. The friends of the bridegroom, you see, don't speak their own voice, but they rejoice at the voice of the bridegroom (see John 3:29). That is why he feeds when they feed, and he says "I feed" because it is his voice in them, his love in them. . . . This is feeding Christ; this is feeding for Christ; this is feeding in Christ — not feeding oneself apart from Christ. . . . So let them all be in the one Shepherd, and speak with the one voice of the Shepherd, which the sheep may hear and follow.[32]

Far from being a potential source of conflict, the relationship between human shepherds and Christ the one Shepherd is absolutely central to their identity and work, just as it is for the vocation of all Christians. Again, Amma Sarah stresses that true pastoral authority always dwells in Christ, as it protects and builds up the flock; whereas wicked and unfaithful leaders are always separated from Christ, and they destroy the church for which Christ gave his life. On this matter the scriptures and the witnesses of the early church are again of one mind.

Christians naturally look to their leaders as representatives of Christ, regardless of how their churches officially define the pastoral office. This is not because church leaders possess divine authority on their own — God forbid! — but because, if they are being faithful to their calling, they dwell in Christ and Christ in them. Those who fear the abuses of authority can take comfort in the knowledge that, because church leaders represent the Lord of the whole church, the baptized are given the important role of discerning whether they are being properly fed by a true shepherd or misled by a false one. Christian people rightly expect to find divine grace being administered through their leaders — what else should they hope to find? But they are also in a position to know when their leaders are providing anything other than the healing grace of Christ.

Augustine is again one of our best teachers in this regard. As a pastor he was remarkably transparent about his own lack of authority apart from Christ. In another sermon on the anniversary of his ordination he declares,

> I feed you on what I am fed on myself. I am just a servant; I am not the head of the house *(paterfamilias)*. I set food before you from the pantry that I too live on, from the Lord's storerooms, from the banquet of that householder who "for our sakes became poor, though he was rich, in order to enrich us from his poverty" (2 Cor. 8:9).[33]

Just as Christ is the one true Shepherd, so he is also the only real teacher of all Christians. On another occasion Augustine tells his congregation,

> Your love knows that we all have but one teacher, and that under him we are fellow disciples. We bishops are not your teachers simply because we speak to you from a higher place, but it is the one who dwells in all of us who is the teacher of us all.[34]

Gregory Nazianzen too emphasizes that pastors administer the same grace that God has conferred on his people since creation and the institution of the covenants: "Of this same healing, we who are set over others are the ministers and fellow-laborers."[35] Christ is not only the devotional focus of the church's life and the goal toward which pastors are guiding their flocks; he is always the source, the standard, and the primary agent of that ministry.

Difficulty and Delight

Every working pastor knows only too well that church leadership is freighted with myriad demands on our time and attention. Many leaders feel a sense of frustration that they are pulled every which way by busywork and interruptions that keep them from doing the things they first entered the ministry to do: preaching, teaching, pastoral care, study, prayer, and liturgical leadership. They are right to feel frustrated. The real question, however, is why we allow this to happen and whether we do anything about it. There are many important jobs that need doing in a Christian community, but it is the ordained pastoral leaders, often together with designated lay leaders, who are uniquely commissioned with overseeing the spiritual growth and well-being of the flock. Above all, pastoral leaders are moral and spiritual guides in the Christian life, and it is they who are chiefly responsible for leading people toward God in Christ by the power of the Holy Spirit. If the appointed leaders of the church do not maintain this primary focus, the spiritual state of the community will languish.

The challenge of staying focused on our primary responsibilities is hardly new. Ours is certainly not the first generation of clergy to feel overwhelmed with administering large organizations, balancing budgets, and attending meetings while we struggle to make time for study, prayer, and sermon preparation. As a diocesan bishop, Augustine was occupied with the administration of a cathedral staff, caring for the needs of widows, orphans, and the poor, advocating for prisoners and those on death row, arbitrating lawsuits, ransoming those who had been kidnapped, supervising assistant bishops in the surrounding towns, a substantial amount of travel for visitations and church councils — not to mention years of engagement in theological disputes against Donatists and Pelagians. Yet, at the same time, he prayed and studied the scriptures; he preached sermons that were far from inferior, often several times a week; and he managed to find time, in the midst of it all, to write such works as *Confessions, The City of God,* and *The Trinity!* As busy as he was, Augustine kept his focus on the chief work of leadership, which is the spiritual guidance of the faithful.

The difficulties of pastoral work are not limited to problems of time management. The spiritual guidance of Christ's flock is a weighty task, to put it mildly. The consequences of our work are eternal, both for our flock and for ourselves, and the sorts of opposition that we face can be daunting. The difficulty of church leadership is one of the recurring themes of early pastoral literature — so much so, in fact, that every one of the major early pastoral theologians sought to avoid priestly office in one way or another, on account of its challenges and burdens.[36] Augustine himself wanted to avoid the pastorate so badly that he stayed away from any church that lacked a bishop, lest he be made one! He was finally caught in the church of Hippo (which still had a bishop), when the congregation acclaimed Augustine as their next leader. Seizing the moment, Bishop Valerius ordained Augustine on the spot as his designated successor.[37] Years later, after much experience as a working bishop, Augustine wrote on the gravity of the pastoral office:

> Every day — indeed every minute of the day, and with unceasing concern — a bishop should ponder what a burden of pastoral responsibility he bears, and what sort of account he will have to render for it to his Lord.[38]

Elsewhere he adds that if one loves Jesus enough to want to feed his sheep, as Peter did, one must be ready to die for the sheep that Jesus bought at the price of his own blood, as he told Peter he would.[39] Augustine therefore asks Christians to pray for their pastors, just as the Apostle Paul asked his churches to do.[40] Gregory the Great takes the matter so seriously that he tells us he wrote his *Pastoral Rule* specifically in order to impress on current and aspiring leaders how difficult and weighty pastoral ministry is. In Gregory's view, if even the saints who were commanded directly by God were afraid, all pastors should have a healthy fear of exercising such authority over others.[41] While it is immensely delightful and satisfying work, it is also important that both leaders and people appreciate how challenging church leadership really is.

When church leaders maintain their focus and exercise their ministry faithfully, the church is well fed and watered, and it thrives abundantly. For those entrusted with pastoral responsibility, to love Christ and to be "in Christ" *is* to feed Christ's sheep.[42] It is this work of guiding people into maturity in Christ, whether they be unbelievers or seasoned Christians, that forms our most basic identity and gives meaning to everything we do. The third-century *Teaching of the Twelve Apostles* gives an excellent summary of this work:

> Honor the bishops, who have loosed you from sins, who by the water regenerated you, who filled you with the Holy Spirit, who reared you with the word as with milk, who bred you up with doctrine, who confirmed you with admonition, and made you to partake of the holy Eucharist of God and made you partakers and joint heirs of the promise of God.[43]

One of the most beautiful descriptions of priestly ministry is found in Gregory Nazianzen's oration on the priesthood:

> The scope of our therapy is to provide the soul with wings — to rescue it from the world and give it to God: to watch over what is in God's image if it abides, to take it

by the hand if it is in danger, or to restore it if it is ruined — to make Christ to dwell in the heart by the Spirit, and in short to deify and bestow heavenly bliss on those who have pledged their allegiance to heaven [in baptism].[44]

Pastoral ministry is a kind of healing treatment, or "cure of souls," by which the habits, commitments, loves, and desires of believers are transformed into ones that reflect the nature and will of God more fully. It is regularly shaped by the study of the scriptures and a life of prayer, which make it a deeply theological enterprise. In the fullest sense, it is a participation in the life of the Holy Trinity, as one of the key forms of Christian life brought into being and sustained by God, and it is ultimately the Trinity that creates and gives meaning to all church leadership. Finally, church leadership is exercised most regularly through the "distribution of the word," as Gregory calls it, through preaching, teaching, personal counsel, and the celebration of the mysteries of the church. But in the most immediate sense, church leadership draws on the pastor's own spiritual life — on our knowledge of God and our real experience of the grace of Christ in the power of the Spirit. It is to the priest's character of holiness that we turn next.

II

Spirituality for Leadership

Set the believers an example in speech and conduct, in love, in faith, in purity. . . . Pay close attention to yourself and to your teaching; continue in these things, for in doing this you will save both yourself and your hearers.

1 Timothy 4:12, 16

People bring many different gifts and talents to the work of church leadership. At times these personal qualities can seem particularly attractive to pastors and churchgoers alike, and some clergy deployment programs are designed to match the right set of gifts with the stated needs of the community. Yet the kind of leadership that feeds the church in real and lasting ways is based on a different sort of charisma altogether. What ultimately moves people into a deeper life in Christ is not personal charm, social connections, or managerial expertise, no matter how useful they may seem in the short term. Instead it is the real and palpable holiness of a leader steeped in the grace of Christ.

What makes us authentic and compelling leaders is a kind of spiritual magnetism that comes not from our natural gifts alone, but from the power of God. True shepherds of the church radiate Christ's grace and holiness in their thoughts, words, and deeds. For this reason, pastors are sometimes compared to icons: they are to be visible and tangible manifestations of God's grace to the church, so that they can lead people into deeper relationship with Christ through the instrumentality of their lives.

Gregory of Nyssa wrote to the church in Nicomedia when it was recovering from a leadership crisis and was about to elect a new bishop. The Nicomedians were familiar with the trappings of worldly power since their city was only recently the eastern capital of the Roman Empire, before the founding of Constantinople. Perhaps for this very reason Gregory tells the Nicomedians that their new bishop's "spiritual qualifications" will be far more important than a prestigious family lineage, wealth, powerful friends, or worldly distinction. If they truly desire a wise and strong leader, they must choose a person who has "a single eye to the things of God." The apostles, after all, were not military or government officials; they were not distinguished with elite education or rhetorical training or membership in the learned professions. And yet, with God's grace in abundance, they were richer than the most pompous Roman senator or wealthy satrap of Mesopotamia, and their message spread to all the earth. The most powerful church leaders are those who are "great according to God's standard," whatever their worldly endowments may be. In conclusion Gregory proposes a wonderful metaphor: what does it matter how magnificent the aqueduct is for those who are thirsty, if there is no water in it? What the church needs is fresh spring water, even if it flows through a wooden pipe.[1]

Contrary to what we may expect, the most powerful and practical resource that church leaders have at their disposal, week in and week out, is their own knowledge and experience of God. The most valuable asset for pastoral ministry is one's own spirituality. Far above any particular skill or expertise, even more important than education or management technique, the most crucial prerequisite for church leadership is the pastor's holiness and life in Christ. Whatever other skills we may bring to pastoral ministry God will no doubt use in surprising ways, but it is our life in Christ that makes for effective ministry in the deepest and most lasting sense. Without this divine gift, no other personal attribute or worldly qualification will amount to anything in the end.

The Order of the Spirit

The scriptures and the early saints repeatedly stress that, in order to guide others in Christ, church leaders must be acquainted with Christ themselves and know his healing grace in their own lives. Gregory the Great asks poignantly,

> How could anyone who does not know himself to be in the intimacy of God's grace, through the merits of his life, presume to usurp the role of intercessor before God on behalf of the people? How can anyone possibly ask for the forgiveness of another when he does not know that he himself has been reconciled?[2]

To attempt to lead others in the Christian life without having advanced in that life is not merely unadvisable or difficult; it is in fact impossible, not to mention hypocritical and destructive of the faith of others. Yet how easy it can be, in the busyness of active ministry, to overlook our most central work, which is to know and love God, so that we may adequately feed others.

The way to prepare for and sustain a vital pastoral ministry, therefore, is to follow what Gregory Nazianzen calls "the order of the Spirit."³ Who would think of teaching a musical instrument, Gregory asks, without first learning how to play? Or who would presume to captain a ship who hasn't first handled the oar, taken the helm, and had some experience of the wind and sea?⁴ We must first surrender to the Spirit and allow ourselves to be transformed by it in order to communicate God's grace to others.⁵ Having entered deeply into this process of transformation, a candidate for priest or bishop is then anointed with the Holy Spirit and the oil of chrism in the ordination rite — is literally "made a christ" — and is entrusted with the Spirit to lead and guide God's people.⁶ At his own ordination to the episcopate Gregory explicitly dedicated himself to the Spirit, in hopes of becoming "an instrument of God, an instrument of the Word tuned and plucked by the Spirit," and hence able to minister to his congregation as a musician plays a many-stringed lyre.⁷ In the order of the Spirit, it is those who are being sanctified by the grace of Christ who are in a position to lead others. This principle runs like a refrain through Gregory's works: only those who are being purified are in a position to cleanse others.⁸ Simply put, "Those whom God appoints to lead his people must be distinguished above all by their virtue,"⁹ and only a ministry that is based in Christian virtue constitutes a "pastoral method" worthy of Christ, the true Shepherd.¹⁰

Regrettably, however, it is not always so. There have been many who sought leadership authority without the basic knowledge of Christ. Gregory confronts church leaders with this central question:

> Do you think talking about God is important? It is more important to purify yourself for God. . . . Do you think teaching is important? It is safer to be a disciple! . . . Why do you make yourself a shepherd when you are a sheep? . . . But if you are mature in Christ and your "fac-

ulties have been trained" (Heb. 5:14) and the light of your knowledge is bright, *then* pronounce the wisdom of God that is spoken among the perfect and is secret and hidden (1 Cor. 2:6-7) as you receive it and it has been entrusted to you.[11]

Only those who are being transformed by the very precepts that they teach are even aware of the meaning of their own words. Amma Syncletica likewise urges that it is dangerous for anyone to provide pastoral guidance who has not first been formed in his or her own life with Christ.[12]

Pastoral ministry depends on the trust that people place in their leaders, and what inspires trust more than anything else is the leader's own spirit of holiness. Only leaders who are truly holy, Gregory the Great writes, will move the laity to trust them "as a crying child seeks its mother's breast."[13] People are inclined to trust their souls to those who are "well-skilled to soften them by the fervent heat of the Holy Spirit," Gregory of Nyssa writes.[14] Again, Ambrose asks,

> Who is going to entrust himself to someone whose wisdom seems to be no greater than his own, when he is the one wanting advice? . . . When it comes to obtaining good advice, it is uprightness of life, an obvious preference for the virtues, a reliable goodwill, and a pleasant and courteous manner that are the qualities that matter most. After all, who looks for a spring in a patch of mud? Who wants to quench his thirst with dirty water?[15]

If the same holds for all Christians in their relations with the world, how much more so does it apply to the leaders of the church?

Augustine is characteristically frank with his congregation about his own need for holiness:

> Because of the duty assigned to us we guard you, brothers and sisters, but our desire is to be guarded by God along with you. We act as your shepherds, but with you we are sheep under the one Shepherd. We stand in this elevated position as your instructors, but we are also your fellow-students in this school under our one Teacher.[16]

The first rule of church leadership is that we must keep our focus on God and the things of God above all. Again, this may seem obvious, but it is in fact an extremely demanding project, given the challenges and responsibilities of the office and the many other things that vie for our attention. When people look at us, they need to see the light of Christ shining in our own lives first, without which everything else we do will ultimately be a sham. Only by being students of how to live will we be able to "irrigate the arid hearts of our neighbors with flowing streams of doctrine," as Gregory the Great beautifully says.[17] Gregory devotes the first book of his *Pastoral Rule* to the subject of pastoral holiness, because it is the place where we must begin to understand our ministry. John Chrysostom too writes that the priesthood is an office that needs the virtue of an angel, and "the soul of a priest should shine like a light beaming over the whole world."[18] The basis of our pastoral authority, and of everything we do, is our own life in Christ. It is no accident that Paul regularly told his churches what many great leaders have said ever since: "Be imitators of me, as I am of Christ" (1 Cor. 11:1).[19]

Pastoral Virtue

The saying is sure: whoever aspires to the office of bishop desires a noble task. Now a bishop must be above re-

proach, married only once, temperate, sensible, respectable, hospitable, an apt teacher, not a drunkard, not violent but gentle, not quarrelsome, and not a lover of money. He must manage his own household well, keeping his children submissive and respectful in every way — for if someone does not know how to manage his own household, how can he take care of God's church? He must not be a recent convert, or he may be puffed up with conceit and fall into the condemnation of the devil. Moreover, he must be well thought of by outsiders, so that he may not fall into disgrace and the snare of the devil.

1 Timothy 3:1-7

Everything that we have said thus far applies to the spiritual life of church leaders in the most basic sense: we are to possess the cardinal virtues of faith, hope, and love, which we share with all of our fellow Christians. As Ambrose says, Christian faith and wisdom is the "source from which all the other virtues derive."[20] In short, clergy are expected to be holy people. Note this does not mean that all holy people should be clergy or official lay leaders. Holiness is the basic vocation of all Christians, to which we constantly aspire. But it is particularly crucial that church leaders be mature Christians and not new converts, as we read in 1 Timothy 3. Pastoral work is far too demanding for an unstable, new believer to manage responsibly and with humility without being tempted to rely on his or her human strength alone. Visible personal holiness is an essential requirement for aspiring and practicing pastoral leaders.

Yet besides faith, hope, and love, there are other virtues that are needed in the pastoral office. Much of early Christian literature on the subject takes the form of commentary on 1 Timothy 3, where the particular requirements of a bishop are spelled out. One of the most striking things about this list of virtues is how social they are. The quality listed first and last is that a bishop must have a good reputation both within the church and in the wider community. This is not because ministry is a popularity contest; it is because leadership is a preeminently social occupation, and in order to function well leaders must be truly respected by others. A bishop or pastor also represents the entire community (again, regardless of a church's official doctrines on the matter), so his or her esteem reflects the honor of the entire community; whereas a leader of ill repute will bring shame to the community. The public esteem of church leaders must be maintained in every way, through personal generosity and hospitality, a temperate disposition, good sense, sobriety, and financial integrity.[21]

As 1 Timothy specifies, this includes the management of our familial relationships. In one sense, our intimate relationships are private and need to be protected from exposure to overly curious communities — and, we should add, from leaders who are overly eager to enjoy the cheap familiarity of sharing family stories or other information that should be kept private. But there is another sense in which family relationships are public, which is symbolized by the liturgical celebration of a wedding. In their public dimension, our family relationships are very much part of the persona and "leadership profile" of a pastor. While it is certainly possible (and regrettably common) for communities or leaders themselves to violate the privacy and health of leaders' families, it is also possible to err in the opposite direction, by imagining that our relationships are in no sense the business of others. But if pastoral authority is based on real virtue and holiness, then the condition of our relationships is directly relevant to the work of ministry. For the holiness of Christ must shine through our relationships, just as in every other area of our life.

The charge to have well-managed relationships does not mean that our families will never have any problems. All families face difficulties, and to pretend otherwise only makes matters worse. What is critical for our ability to lead the church is the way that we deal with the challenges that life inevitably brings. Again, that is often easier said than done. For this reason it is helpful for leaders to admit to themselves how tempting it can be, when things are difficult at home, to escape the hard work of family love by seeking the gratification and approval that comes from our work at church. But this is the wrong choice for our families and for the church. Christianity is a religion of healing and redemption, and, as 1 Timothy states, it is not possible to lead the church if we ourselves are not seeking and receiving God's grace in every area of our lives. For leaders who have immediate families, they are the most intimate relationships that we have, and if we are not allowing God to illuminate that part of our life in particular, then we are living in darkness in a profound way, no matter how many other public virtues we may display. Family relationships are by definition both private and public, and the maintenance of their health is central to the work of church leadership.

Gregory the Great gives a memorable list of virtues at the beginning of his treatment of the pastor's life. A church leader must be

> pure in thought, exemplary in conduct, discerning in silence, profitable in speech, a compassionate neighbor to everyone, anxious in contemplation for the sake of others, an ally of those who live well in humility, and firm in the zeal of righteousness against the vices of sinners. He must not relax his care for the internal life while he is occupied by external concerns, nor should he relinquish what is prudent of external matters in order to focus on things internal.[22]

Perhaps the most necessary single quality for leadership is that one must be able to teach Christian doctrine persuasively and to oppose falsehood. Augustine repeatedly says that the chief responsibility of a bishop is to be a faithful teacher of apostolic doctrine, and on this point he speaks for the other major early theologians as well. We will consider the important work of Christian teaching in the last chapter.

There is one pastoral virtue that deserves our careful attention here, because of its centrality to the pastor's spirituality as well as its constant difficulty — that of humility and gentleness. First Peter gives a classic apostolic statement:

> I exhort the presbyters among you to tend the flock of God. . . . Do not lord it over those in your charge, but be examples to the flock. . . . Clothe yourselves with humility in your dealings with one another, for "God opposes the proud, but gives grace to the humble" (Prov. 3:34). Humble yourselves, therefore, under the mighty hand of God, so that he may exalt you in due time. 1 Pet. 5:1-6

Humility is a crucial virtue for church leaders for several reasons. As we noted in the previous chapter, pastors carry real authority in people's lives simply by virtue of their office. Our power is so great, and the matters that we deal with are of such consequence, that we must be especially careful to remain humble as we exercise our ministry. Because of the deep needs that people bring to the church they will simply not trust church leaders if they perceive that we bear any malice toward them or are in it for our own glory. Similarly, it can be offensive and off-putting when church leaders are sour, bitter, or sarcastic with their flocks. To be sure, pastors are called to admonish their flocks firmly when necessary, but this is a work of love that requires self-sacrifice and a desire to build others up, and it should never be an effort to elevate ourselves at the expense of others.

There are other reasons why humility is so important,

which have to do with how the exercise of leadership affects us as leaders. The experience of providing pastoral guidance to people who truly need it is immensely satisfying. Yet our satisfaction in a job well done can easily shift from joy in people's growth in Christ to a sense of delight in our own power and honor. At this point our leadership becomes more about us than those we are serving, however we may portray it to ourselves and others, and this is both selfish and destructive. Moreover, because we are dealing with people's relationships with God, it can be tempting to claim this profound experience of glory for ourselves. For those who are in a position of spiritual authority, Gregory the Great writes, the heart is easily elated by the real experience of glory.[23] Here we come to an all-too-familiar theme for many pastors: that we often hunger for the approval of others. Again Gregory writes with great insight and honesty,

> The mind of the priest is often seduced by the approval of those below him, and consequently he is exalted beyond himself. While he is outwardly surrounded with immense favor, internally he becomes empty of the truth. Forgetful of who he is, he scatters himself among the voices of others and believes what he hears all around him rather than what he should discern about himself from within.[24]

If we are honest with ourselves, we can all recognize how enticing the approval of others can be. Do we long to hear that the sermon was well liked, the hospital visit appreciated, or the counseling session helpful? It is not a question of whether our ministries should be effective; of course they should. The point is whether we want them to be so in order to glorify God and to serve others, or whether we are in fact seeking our own honor and esteem. Amma Sarah warns that if she were to pray to God that all people would approve of her life, she would immediately need to beg the forgiveness of those whose approval she sought![25] When we seek to promote our own reputation, we "prostitute ourselves to the corrupting spirit in our lust for praise," Gregory adds.[26]

The real trouble with focusing on what others think of us goes to the very heart of our faith. For by doing so we are placing our reputation and even what we may think is the good of other people above the love of God, and so we violate the First Commandment (Mark 12:30; Deut. 6:5). But the love of God must exceed all other allegiances and determine everything we do; not even the good of my neighbor (if I could imagine that apart from God) can take its place. Augustine dwells on this very matter in the first book of *Christian Teaching,* a passage that has had an enormous influence on the history of Christian ethics, but which we should recall was initially written for the benefit of practicing pastoral leaders.[27] Only God deserves the full allegiance of our entire being, Augustine argues, and God is the end of all creaturely life. To be sure, we cannot love God if we do not also love our neighbor, and "if we say that we love God but do not love our brothers and sisters we are liars" (1 John 4:20). But only God can determine what that love consists in, and any attempt to reverse the love of God and neighbor leads to idolatry. The only way to love our neighbor as pastoral leaders, as in the Christian life in general, is to love God first and above all. When we focus on our own honor, however, we love ourselves above both God and our neighbor. The real satisfaction, esteem, and confidence that result from pastoral ministry derive from God, not from us or from the regard of others alone. There is a very big difference between looking to God as the source of our vocational purpose and seeking that validation from others. As John Chrysostom writes, two key things are necessary for good preaching: "the power of preaching well" and "indifference to praise." If either is lacking, he says, the other becomes useless.[28]

In one sense good pastors do want to please people. But Gregory the Great cautions that they must do so only "to lead their neighbors to an affection for the Truth by the sweetness of their own character. It is not because they want to be loved."[29] Obviously people are not going to follow someone they do not love and respect. Church leaders must earn that respect — but solely for the purpose of leading others to Christ; never to attract their esteem for its own sake. There is a great difference between the two, and to seek to be loved per se is in fact to relinquish our leadership. For the same reason we are not friends with our parishioners, in the sense of peers with whom we share an equal footing and can expect to give and receive the goods of friendship. We are servant-leaders, and if we seek to receive from our flocks in the manner of a friend or loved one, we have abandoned our authority and our responsibility to provide guidance as a gift. The matter becomes clearest when we consider the fact that people do not always know or want what they truly need any more than we ourselves do. As pastoral leaders we are interested not in what pleases others, but with what ought to please them, what is truly in their best interest. It takes constant vigilance to know the difference and a kind of neutral detachment in order to act on it.

The real measure of our aims, then, is not to please others but to please Christ, and we please others only in order to lead them to Christ. Paul addresses this dual concern as well. He writes to the Corinthians, "I try to please everyone in everything I do, not seeking my own advantage, but that of [others], so that they may be saved" (1 Cor. 10:33). Yet he speaks even more strongly of pleasing God above all: "If I were still pleasing people, I would not be a servant of Christ" (Gal. 1:10); and, "We speak not to please mortals, but to please God who tests our hearts" (1 Thess. 2:4). Gregory the Great summarizes in very strong terms: "Whoever desires to be loved by members of the church through the good works that he performs rather than by Christ is an enemy of Christ."[30]

In the late fourth century the monastic writer Evagrius of Pontus synthesized the spiritual teachings of the church as they were practiced by monks he visited from Egypt to Asia Minor. Among his writing is the first list of what would come to be known as "the seven deadly sins." Evagrius comments that, among the most dangerous and hurtful sins, the besetting sin of clergy is vainglory. What pastors must strive to avoid more than anything else is their own sense of honor and prestige. John Chrysostom writes in a similar vein that, in order to avoid "the most dangerous rock of vainglory,"[31] the premier virtue of Christian priests must be humility, surpassed only by faith itself. In Chrysostom's words, humility is the "mother, root, nurse, foundation, and bond of all good things" for church leaders.[32] Amma Syncletica of Egypt likewise stresses the importance of humility in the Christian life: "Just as one cannot build a ship unless one has some nails, so it is impossible to be saved without humility."[33] Again, the great monastic teacher Theodora extols the power of humility above all other spiritual practices: more than fasting, vigils, or any other act that one might undertake, only humility can safely guide us on the path of salvation, and it is humility that gives us the power to defeat the snares of the enemy.[34] It takes real spiritual maturity to remain humble as we lead others, which is why 1 Timothy makes a special point about the need for bishops not to be new converts.[35] Contrary to what many think, the mark of humility in a Christian priest is not low self-esteem or a weak personality. Effective pastoral leadership requires much confidence and a comfort with exercising authority in people's lives. Rather, the authentic mark of humility is a clear focus on God, a commitment to the work of ministry, and a heartfelt desire for the spiritual growth of God's people, not for our own glory.

One of the great risks that self-concern poses is that we may seem to be caring for our flocks when in fact we are not. Whatever other successes we may display, they will inevitably serve our own egos or the worldly expectations of others, rather than the actual needs of others. Augustine reflects on the problem in one of his sermons:

> My danger is this, that I might pay attention to how you praise me and take no notice of the sort of lives you lead. But [God] knows, the one under whose gaze I speak — under whose gaze I see that I am not delighted by popular praise so much as I am vexed and troubled about what sort of lives are led by those who praise me! As for being praised by those who lead bad lives, I don't want it — I shudder at it, I detest it, it causes me pain, not pleasure. As for being praised by those who lead good lives, if I say I don't want it I will be lying. If I say I do want it, I'm afraid I may be more bent on vanity than on the solid truth.[36]

Obviously clergy rely on the feedback of their congregation, especially the more reliable members, and we hope this includes some amount of well-deserved praise; otherwise, we're not doing our jobs. The trouble is that we need to hear such praise objectively, so to speak, as valuable information about how we are doing, so that we can minister more effectively. Yet even accurate praise from the right people brings with it the danger of inflating our pride. In another sermon, Augustine admits that he dreads nothing more than the danger of taking more pleasure in the honor that people show him for being a bishop than he does in the actual fruit that they bear for salvation.[37] Even warranted praise can obscure our real goal, which is to build up the church into full maturity in Christ, and so to glorify God rather than ourselves.

One of the most insightful sections of Gregory the Great's *Pastoral Rule* concerns the insidious dynamics of our lust for praise. Indeed, the entire work is aimed at driving church leaders back from "the precipice of their ambition."[38] In his parting words at the end of the work Gregory notes that it is actually when we have ministered most effectively — when we have delivered a powerful sermon, presided at a glorious service for a major feast day, or met the needs of a family in crisis — that we must be especially careful to avoid vainglory. Not only do we hunger for praise when we are unsure how things are going; when we know they are going well, the desire for approval is almost irresistible and threatens to make us prideful rather than grateful, self-satisfied rather than joyful, just when God's grace is most evident. At these times, what Gregory calls "the hidden joys of self-display" can easily catch us off guard.[39] Given the challenge of maintaining humility even in the best of circumstances, Gregory concludes with a confession of his own weakness and a plea for help from his readers:

> Alas, I am like a poor painter trying to paint a handsome person. I am trying to point others to the shore of perfection, when I myself am still tossed by the waves of sin. In the shipwreck of this life, I beg you to sustain me with the chart of your prayers.[40]

Character and Office

Those whom God appoints to lead his people must be distinguished above all by their virtue.

Gregory Nazianzen[41]

One of the recurring dilemmas of church leadership concerns the relationship between spiritual, charismatic authority and the institutional authority that leaders carry by virtue of their office. This dilemma affects most Christian communities in one way or another, regardless of their official doctrine of ministry or the prevailing culture of leadership and power. The pastoral office inevitably carries a kind of official and symbolic authority that precedes and succeeds any particular occupant, and which can, for a time at least, operate almost independently of the leader's character and actions. At some level people look to church leaders for spiritual guidance simply because they hold the office they do. And yet, as we have seen, pastoral leadership is based on far more than institutional authority alone. How then are we to understand the relationship between the two?

It is extremely significant that all of the great early theologians speak strongly against relying on institutional power for one's pastoral authority. Their cautions are all the more striking when we recognize that most of them were heavily invested in formal leadership structures, and in some cases they even welcomed the patronage of the church by the Roman state. Jerome, for example — who was no mild lamb when it came to asserting himself — states very clearly that "the blessedness of a bishop, priest, or deacon does not lie in the fact that they are bishops, priests, or deacons, but in their having the virtues that their names and offices imply."[42] Theodore of Mopsuestia warns that, although pastors carry official authority, they must lead by their character, goodwill, and persuasive teaching alone, since "the discharge of duties in church is not an honor, but a work."[43] Early pastoral literature is replete with similar statements.

Augustine gives a penetrating discussion of the dilemma in *Christian Teaching*. He stresses that, beyond all skills, technique, and effort, what matters most is the pastor's manner of life, as Paul directs in 1 Timothy. Yet Augustine also knows that Paul rejoices in the proclamation of Christ even if it comes from selfish or ulterior motives (Phil. 1:18; 2:21) — that one can "speak wisely and eloquently while living a worthless kind of life," and still provide some real instruction. After all, even Jesus tells his followers to do what the Pharisees say but not what they do (Matt. 23:3).

At the same time, Augustine is keen to note the consequences of unrighteous preaching. First of all, any work that is not based on the character of holiness is of no benefit to ministers themselves, so they are deluding themselves to think that they are gaining anything from it. Whatever true teaching may come from those who live falsely does not even belong to them, he says, but is stolen from others who possess it truly. Secondly, Augustine reminds us that we can't fool all the people all the time. In the long run, "people will not hear and obey someone who does not listen to himself." Unrighteous ministers undermine the effectiveness of the word, cheapen the gospel, and eventually cause people to despise it. How many souls have been led away from the gospel, Augustine asks, by the destructive conduct of one of its ministers? Thirdly, character-based leadership is more effective than empty words. For all these reasons we must, as Paul says, "act well in the sight of God and other people" (2 Cor. 8:21) because our manner of life is itself an eloquent sermon.[44]

The rule of thumb is very simple: institutional authority must always be based on charismatic authority, and the power of the leadership office must reflect one's spiritual condition. In reality the authority of the office *is* the authority of the Holy Spirit, which sanctifies, empowers, and anoints the leaders of the church. It is critically important that the church fathers never say, in effect, "When the going gets tough, just rely on your institutional authority." Not only is such behavior harmful in many ways; it is also directly forbidden by Christ. When Christian bishops came to exercise other forms of leadership in the church and the wider community, their spiritual authority remained the basis of all they did.[45] The reason is easy enough to see in our own experience. Given enough time, most people are either inspired by a leader's grace and holiness or they are repelled by his or her spiritual malaise. In every case, the multiple tasks and forms of authority that pastors engage in should reflect their spiritual or charismatic authority.

True pastoral leaders must therefore relinquish other forms of power, including the prerogatives and the bare symbolism of the office when it lacks a worthy occupant. Clerical authority that has no basis in Christian virtue is a perversion at best and diabolical at worst. Amma Theodora counsels that "a teacher must be a stranger to the desire for domination, vainglory, and pride."[46] Practicing church leaders must be constantly vigilant of their own growth in Christ if they are not to fall prey to the temptation to rely on the power and prestige of office alone. Churches likewise must expect and allow their leaders to attend to their own spiritual lives as the real basis of their effectiveness. And supervisors and pastoral calling committees must seek the qualities of holiness and the love of God above all else in their discernment of whom to recommend for leadership roles, including most positions of lay leadership.

The Tragic Alternative

One of the main reasons why pastoral virtue is so important, of course, is that without it leaders can err in ways that not only hinder their ministries, but are positively harmful to others.[47] Unpleasant though it may be, it is necessary to face the tragic alternative of pastoral vice and wickedness in order to understand fully the need for pastoral holiness. We are not by any means the first generation to face serious problems of clergy misconduct. Yet despite the sensationalism fostered by headline news stories, it is not the more dramatic cases of misbehavior that do the most damage to the church, although they are particularly horrid and traumatic when they do occur. Even more damaging are the mundane, softer forms of unrighteousness that more commonly beset church leadership and sap it of spiritual energy. In communities where leadership has become lukewarm or inert people suffer enormously, often in unrecognized ways, from the absence of the vital spiritual guidance that they need. Pastoral vice is a prime example of what classical theologians defined as evil in the strict sense: the deprivation of a good that ought to be there. The greatest harm done by major and minor forms of clergy misconduct is that the positive leadership that God intends for the church is now missing.

In a moment of particular ire, Gregory of Nazianzus lamented the gross abuses of church leadership that he perceived among his contemporaries:

> The holiest office of all is in danger of becoming the most ridiculous . . . ; for promotion depends not on virtue but on vice, and the thrones go not to the most worthy but the most powerful![48]

There are many other loyalties that can compromise the integrity of one's ministry. Among the most destructive are political maneuvering and power-grabbing, captivation by ecclesiastical or social networks, and partisan infighting. The temptation to rely on such forms of worldly power can be just as great for church leaders as for those in any other profession. Yet the stakes are very high indeed, and the potential for harm can hardly be overstated. Gregory the Great comments, "No one does more harm in the church than one who has the title or rank of holiness and acts perversely."[49]

Gregory Nazianzen provides timeless insight into the deeper power dynamic involved. Only a virtuous priest, he says, is able to lead others by persuasion; every other form of authority amounts to the tyranny of the world.[50] Those who are charged with shepherding Christ's flock must constantly lead by goodwill and spiritual persuasion, based on their exemplary character, and never by force or compulsion. Even though leaders possess great authority within the community, they offer guidance through the magnetic quality of their instruction,[51] for only a leader who shows real virtue is able to guide others by building them up rather than by pushing them around. We have but two options: either we are leading people by the Spirit of God, or we are trying to manipulate and bully them into the gospel. Christ explicitly forbids the latter.

The choice that we face here is so stark and uncompromising because in reality we are involved in a cosmic struggle about the nature of power. Again, we should be clear that the gospel itself is very much about power: "the power of God for salvation for everyone who has faith" (Rom. 1:16). Paul reminds the Corinthians that his ministry among them was not "with plausible words of wisdom, but with a demonstration of the Spirit and of power" (1 Cor. 2:4).[52] There is no neutral space between the power of God and the powers of the world and the devil. It is not a question of whether or not we exercise power, but of which sphere of power we represent. Pastoral leaders are in a position to do either enormous good or serious harm, to be either beneficial or dangerous to their flocks, depending on whether they convey the power of God or some other form of power. There really is no third option.

Regrettably, there are certain offenses that are so damaging to the pastoral relationship, or which indicate the probability of recurring problems, that they make it no longer possible for the offender to remain in a position of leadership.

Here again we must appreciate the social character of leadership. Church leadership it is not a personal right, nor is it fundamentally a vehicle for the fulfillment of one's personal goals. Severely destructive acts such as sexual misconduct, financial embezzlement, or systematic deceit are obviously among the most damaging. How to define disqualifying offenses has been the subject of many a conciliar canon, and it is a question that the authorities in each church must decide. Wherever the line is drawn, we must remember that it is not about whether a penitent offender can be forgiven by God; the grace of Christ is extended to all who turn to him for help, without exception. Rather, we are talking about fitness for leadership, which is another matter entirely. To appreciate the difference, it may be helpful to recall that the famous cases of notorious sinners, like Paul or Augustine, involved repentance and personal transformation *before* they became leaders in the church. Because the sole purpose of leadership is to build up the church, the community's interests are always paramount in the handling of extreme clergy misconduct.

The early fathers are again unanimous on the subject of pastoral abuse, and we need to hear their admonition soberly. "How many wrecks of churches, people and all, have taken place as a result of the inexperience of their heads!" Gregory of Nyssa laments.[53] Gregory Nazianzen writes that an incompetent priest or bishop is nothing short of an outrage to the Christian mystery.[54] Augustine speaks with equal force, commenting on Ezekiel 34:3-5:

"How do they kill [God's people]?" you say. By leading bad lives, by setting a bad example. . . . Even a strong sheep often enough, when he notices his pastor leading a bad life, if his eyes wander from the rules of the Lord and are attracted by human considerations, begins to say to himself, "If my pastor lives like that, who am I not to behave as he does?" . . . The pastor who lives a bad life openly in the sight of the people is killing as many people as he is observed by.[55]

No matter how challenging our work may be, we are never permitted to employ the tyranny of the world in place of God's grace. None of the apostles or early church leaders is prepared to allow any excuse for such behavior, for the souls and bodies of God's people are at stake.

It is difficult for everyone involved when serious misconduct occurs on the part of any church leader, lay or ordained. On the one hand, we know that believers are not excused by the behavior of their leaders. All Christians must strive to obey what their pastors say, if not what they do, as Jesus said of the Pharisees (Matt. 23:3). And yet, on the other hand, it is imperative to acknowledge that harm is being done and to find a way to confront it, however discomforting that may be. Christians must be as realistic as they can about their leaders, and strive to be neither fawning nor cynical about them. Augustine complains that some people see only good among the clergy and refuse to admit that there are bad ones as well, while others are critical of all leaders because of the sins of a few. Of course both views are wrong.[56] The fact that some abuse the pastoral office makes it all the more important that leaders and people alike continue planting the seeds of faith. After all, Augustine observes, farmers and gardeners continue to plant even when some seeds fail to grow, or ants and birds carry them off.

> So we do not cease to work in the church, which is like the field of a great landowner. But it is up to God to give the increase, because, even if all do not make progress and persevere up to the end, the Lord nonetheless

knows those who are his, as the apostle says (2 Tim. 2:19). He foretold the coming of all these scandals that cause us sadness. He warned that we should not give up, and he promised a reward to us who persevere with his help. . . . So place your hope in God, my children and brothers and sisters, and let your love not grow cold, so that you may be found with proven virtue on the last day.[57]

There is always reason for faith, hope, and love, even when some abuse their authority. Nevertheless church leaders may *never* make the same excuse for themselves. Those who claim that the laity ought to follow what they say but not what they do, so they can lead bad lives and rely on their official authority alone, are not real shepherds, but vicious imposters. Augustine warns, "If they were real shepherds, they would never say such things!" Only those who "preach God because they love God, who preach God for God's sake," are real shepherds and not "hired hands."[58] Given the dangers involved, it is no surprise that spiritual writers of every generation have emphasized the need for constant repentance on the part of church leaders. Repentance is the way to holiness for all Christians, but it is especially necessary for the leaders of the church.

All from God

We have this treasure in jars of clay, so that it may be clear that this extraordinary power belongs to God and does not come from us.

2 Corinthians 4:7

The admonitions to pastoral holiness in scripture and early Christian tradition show us the true character and basis of church leadership. Only by leading in this way can we ensure that our ministries rest on the grace of God and not our own power. If to some this looks like a form of works righteousness, the opposite is in fact the case. It is when we are *not* leading from the power and holiness of Christ that we are falsifying our ministries and deriving our authority from some other source. As the work of Augustine shows, the principle of holiness in church leadership stands firmly against the heresy of Pelagianism, against which he labored so vehemently in the final decades of his life. In order for our ministries to be effective, the virtue of church leaders must be real; but true virtue comes only from Christ.

This means that pastoral leaders dwell in the Christian paradox of strength in weakness. Augustine gives a beautiful depiction of this in his commentary on Psalm 65:6: "Preparing mountains in his strength, he is girdled about with might." Augustine compares the mountains to the leaders of God's people:

> "Preparing mountains in *his* strength" — not in their own strength. God prepared great preachers, and called them mountains: they were lowly in their own eyes, but towering in him. . . . What did one of those mountains say? "In ourselves we found nothing but the token of death, to ensure that we should put our trust not in ourselves, but in God, who raises the dead" (2 Cor. 1:9). Anyone who trusts in himself and not in Christ is not one of those mountains that God prepares in his strength.[59]

To be a strong and effective leader is to remain constantly humble before God, and whenever we elevate ourselves apart from God we are no longer real leaders. Only by remaining profoundly uninterested in our own glory can we dwell in God's grace and cease to rely on the power of the world.

If the requirement of holiness for pastoral leaders is not a mark of Pelagianism, neither is it an indication of Donatism, the other major target of Augustine's mature years. Augustine argued against the Donatists that the church's sacraments are not dependent on the moral state of the celebrant; otherwise, how could there ever be a valid sacrament? On this point the Eastern fathers are also in agreement. But, like the other early saints, he is equally insistent that only the holiness of the church's ministers enables them to be effective pastors and to guide people in Christ. As we noted above, those who try to speak wisely while they live wickedly inhibit their ministries in multiple ways. As much as Augustine resisted Donatist claims to a purely righteous ministry, and therefore an exclusively valid church, he labored with even greater zeal in exhorting both clergy and people to lead holy lives.

We should add that pastoral holiness is also not a form of moral rigorism, which in the early church was associated with the movement called Novatianism.[60] The fathers never assume that church leaders will be absolutely perfect; what they require is that they be growing in Christ through repentance and sanctification. As with the saints in general, the holiest of leaders are those who confess how great their sin is — even if, in the eyes of others, it is God's goodness that shines through most clearly. Pastoral holiness is marked by a life of repentance and striving for greater purity, not by having fully arrived, which none of us will do until the final Day of the Lord. The standard of pastoral holiness, then, is not rigorist; it is honest, real, and the only safe and effective way to lead God's church.

III

The Cure of Souls

The leadership of men and women, the craftiest and most complicated of all creatures, seems to me the art of arts and the science of sciences.

Gregory of Nazianzus[1]

A mong the many demands that leaders face, the main purpose of pastoral ministry is to guide people toward God in Christ by the power of the Holy Spirit. Everything that we do as leaders should reflect this purpose. All our work of administration, planning, socializing, and even presiding and preaching at worship is focused on helping people to come to know and love God more fully.

Surprising as it may sound, the work of ministry is essentially the same whether we are dealing with people who do not yet know Christ or believers who are growing in faith. No matter whom we encounter, our aim is to lead people to God in Christ. It is helpful to recall that in the New Testament and the early church, salvation is understood as something that will take place at the end of time, as a result of Christ's final judgment and deliverance of his people (see 1 Thess. 5:8-10;

Rom. 5:9-10). Christians are already justified by faith in Christ's blood, and they hope to *be* saved one day, when Christ returns. Meanwhile, there is always room to grow. We will never meet someone who lives a static existence, and there is no such thing as what some have called a "maintenance" model of ministry. People are either growing toward God or away from God; there is no fixed, middle position. At times we may feel like we are not growing, or that God is absent from us, but such feelings are difficult to interpret, and they do not always mean that we are falling away. Far more dangerous is the complacent belief that we are holding ground and "doing fine" on our own, which is almost certainly a sign that we are turning away from God. Everywhere we turn, we will find people in need of spiritual guidance to draw them closer to Christ, and the focus of church leadership is to provide that guidance.

Gregory Nazianzen describes the work of a bishop as being constantly devoted to this spiritual transformation. Pastoral ministry is "the service and ministry of the Spirit, the strengthening of the people, the governance of souls, and teaching through word, deed, and example 'with the weapons of righteousness' (2 Cor. 6:7)." In order to lead people to God, the pastor

> dedicates them to the Spirit, casts out the darkness, glories in the light, drives away predators, draws together the fold, guards against precipices and desert solitudes, and helps it to reach the mountains and high places.[2]

John Chrysostom writes that our main concern is with the Body of Jesus, which is the church, to "train it to perfect health and incredible beauty," making it worthy of Christ, its Head.[3] This work is more difficult and involved than it may appear at first. Chrysostom is quick to add that the Body of

Christ falls prey to even more diseases than our human bodies do. In order to care for the church pastoral leaders therefore need divine wisdom and an understanding of "the treatment suitable for the soul." What is this spiritual "treatment" that the saints so often speak about? While physicians have medicinal and environmental treatments that they can apply, spiritual physicians have only "teaching by word of mouth" to apply the needed remedies. When it is administered rightly, the pastor's healing speech is extremely effective.

> It is the best instrument, the only diet, and the superior climate. It takes the place of medicine and cautery and surgery. . . . Without it all else is useless. By it we rouse the soul's lethargy or reduce its inflammation, we remove excrescences and supply defects, and, in short, do everything that contributes to its health.[4]

Gregory Nazianzen puts it even more clearly:

> In one thing does the work of a priest lie, and only one: the purification of souls through his life and doctrine. . . . He sends up pure offerings for his children, until the day he makes them into a perfect offering. Other matters should be left to those who are capable of dealing with them.[5]

The transforming "cure of souls" lies at the heart of church leadership. Everything that we do must serve this end.

The Art of Arts

Since the writing of the Old Testament, the leadership of God's people has been described using several key metaphors. We have already noted the primary image of shepherding sheep; also common in biblical and patristic literature, appearing in the prophets and in the teaching of Jesus himself, is that of mending, healing, and restoring individual and social life. In a famous scene Jesus rebukes the scribes and the Pharisees by saying, "Those who are well have no need of a physician, but those who are sick; I have come to call not the righteous but sinners" (Mark 2:17). Jesus not only restored people to physical health, "healing the sick," but he described his entire ministry as that of a spiritual physician. In the realm of the spirit sickness and healing are, in an important sense, not metaphors at all. The maladies of the human mind and heart can be just as debilitating as those of the body, and often more so. Many a poet and sage has voiced the common human experience that the sufferings of the soul can be much harder to bear than sufferings of the body, difficult as those may be.

Echoing these earlier traditions, Gregory Nazianzen famously describes pastoral ministry as "the cure of souls,"[6] and he give the most comprehensive account of pastoral healing in patristic literature.[7] In order to highlight the distinctive nature of pastoral ministry, Gregory compares pastoral healing with the medical treatment of bodies. He distinguishes pastoral ministry in terms of its object, the unique kind of work that it involves, and the ultimate goal of its efforts. The focus of pastoral ministry is on what the Bible and later traditions call the soul.[8] By "soul" we mean the center of a person's life — our values, commitments, and choices, our thoughts and feelings, our memories and hopes for the future.[9] Focusing on human souls does not mean that we are unconcerned with the well-being of the body and the other mundane aspects of human life — quite the contrary. The healing and growth of the soul ("growing into the full stature of Christ") very much involves the body — most especially what we *do* with our bodies, either showing love for God and our neighbor or not (see 1 Cor. 6:15-20) — and the soul's health holds the potential to benefit the body to a surprising degree. Moreover, through the resurrection of the body, the faith, hope, and love that stem from the soul can provide the body with eternal life.

At the same time it is clear that attention to the material and bodily concerns of life is incomplete from the point of view of the gospel. "One does not live by bread alone," Jesus tells the devil who was tempting him to break his fast, "but by every word that comes from the mouth of God" (Matt. 4:4, quoting Deut. 8:3). Later Jesus adds, "Do not fear those who can kill the body but cannot kill the soul; rather fear the one who can destroy both soul and body in hell" (Matt. 10:28),[10] even as he goes on to speak of God's minute care for the body: "Even the hairs of your head are all counted. So do not be afraid; you are of more value than many sparrows" (vv. 30-31). Paul too writes, "Flesh and blood will not inherit the kingdom of God" (1 Cor. 15:50), and yet our mortal bodies will one day put on immortality in the resurrection of the dead (v. 53). The connections between the soul and the body are very close and complex, yet our ministry aims at the soul above all.

In contrast with the treatment of bodies the cure of souls promises a more far-reaching reward. Gregory notes that, while physical medicine can restore the body from disease, the body will inevitably die anyway, however long we may prolong biological life.[11] Pastoral treatment, on the other hand, heals the soul by turning it from the world and the devil and bringing it to God, and it is the condition of the soul that determines whether we will have eternal life with Christ. In the long run, and often in the short run as well, the treatment of the soul stands to benefit most both body and soul. This is one of the reasons why it is so important for church leaders to remain focused on the primary matters of spiritual ministry and not to get caught up in tasks that mainly have to do with people's material needs, for which they will do best to seek help elsewhere. Paradoxically, physical well-being and the greatest society imaginable, in the heavenly Jerusalem, await those who first save their souls.

For those who serve as pastoral ministers on a daily basis it will be obvious how distinctive the work of pastoral treatment is compared with medical care. Physical medicine deals with ailments which, by comparison with spiritual ones, are visible and more directly treatable. Pastoral treatment, however, deals with the deepest and most hidden aspects of our lives: our thoughts and feelings, the habitual and often unconscious ways we act and react to things, our underlying values and commitments — which is to say our wills, or the moral and spiritual direction of our lives.[12] It focuses on what 1 Peter calls "the hidden person of the heart" (1 Pet. 3:4) in order to address the deeper source and the real cause of our spiritual malaise.[13] As Gregory the Great comments, "the afflictions of the mind are more hidden than the wounds of the body."[14] The life of the human spirit is notoriously obscure, complicated, and resistant to change. To motivate people for real and deep change is more difficult than leaders and people often appreciate.

Spiritual guidance is difficult for several reasons. First of all, it takes time to discern where people's growing points are. Moreover, people tend to resist being treated in their inmost thoughts and feelings, particularly when they have been built up with years of habit. If it were easy to address such things, wouldn't they have changed by now? Even our most enthusiastic parishioners can work to avoid their growing points. Gregory Nazianzen is especially perceptive in this regard. Speaking for many pastors before and since, he laments that so many people resist spiritual treatment with the very zeal that they should have for welcoming it. Absurd as it may seem, well-meaning Christians often seek to avoid what Gregory calls "the medicines of wisdom,"[15] despite the fact that such behavior is ultimately self-destructive. Tradition and human experience show only too well that we possess uncanny abilities to deceive ourselves and to obstruct positive growth and change. Some people hide their sins and weaknesses; others make excuses and give elaborate explanations to themselves and others; still others boldly parade their faults. Whether out of cleverness, selfishness, cowardice, or fear, the many ways that people resist pastoral guidance can make our work exceedingly difficult.

As if human wiles were not enough of a challenge, pastoral leaders also face the opposition of the devil, who afflicts people and drives them further into the grips of sin and death. Amma Syncletica warns, "Many are the wiles of the devil": whether we exist in wealth or poverty, sickness or health, the devil will find some way to tempt us.[16] Most insidious of all, Gregory observes, the devil "uses us as his own weapons," turning us against ourselves and causing us to treat those who care about us as if they were our enemies. As the prophet Amos says, "They hate the one who reproves in the gate, and they abhor the one who speaks the truth" (Amos 5:10). Such people "imagine that they are consuming the flesh of others when they are really devouring their own," Gregory adds.[17] It is not uncommon to find individuals and whole communities who are suffering from this kind of moral and spiritual disorder, and when we do it can seem like a form of madness. To some extent this is to be expected as the regular lot of church leaders — not order and harmony, but spiritual chaos and rebellion, the sort of irrational and often inexplicable ways of living that the ancients called *pathos.* In light of these multiple obstacles, pastoral leadership can be extremely challenging, and it is not surprising that Gregory, Augustine, and many others have commented that it is much easier to be led than it is to lead![18] On the other hand, as difficult as pastoral treatment is, it is all the more worthwhile and beneficial when it is practiced well.[19]

The Cure of Souls

The cure of souls represents the basic "method" of pastoral ministry. As an art and a science, church leadership is a distinctive craft (in Greek, a *techne*), with a particular method and sense of expertise. It is also a practical skill rooted in a body of knowledge, much like medicine, law, or government. Most people assume that the work of doctors, lawyers, financial managers, and governors is important. Who would want to go to a doctor who didn't know what he or she was doing? How much more, then, should people expect professional expertise from the leaders of God's church?

In order to lead people in Christ church leaders must administer God's transforming grace in such a way that meets the different needs of people in a wide variety of circumstances. It is here that the basic method (in Greek, the *logos*) of pastoral ministry lies. Paul describes this method in his First Letter to the Corinthians:

> To the Jews I became a Jew in order to win Jews. . . . To those outside the law I became as one outside the law . . . so that I might win those outside the law. To the weak I became weak, so that I might win the weak. I have become all things to all people, that I might by all means save some. I do it all for the sake of the gospel, so that I may share in its blessings. (1 Cor. 9:20-23)

Again, Paul tells the Thessalonians to care for one another in a similar way: "We urge you, beloved, to admonish the idlers, encourage the faint hearted, help the weak, be patient with all of them" (1 Thess. 5:14). This pattern of responsive and adaptive care mirrors the ministry of Jesus himself, who healed the sick, delivered the possessed, and rebuked insolent religious leaders according to the needs of each.[20]

Anyone who undertakes pastoral ministry will soon recognize that the people they are serving exist in many different conditions and situations. Gregory Nazianzen puts the matter clearly:

> Men and women, young and old, rich and poor, the confident and the despondent, the sick and whole, rulers and ruled, the wise and the ignorant, the cowardly and the courageous, the wrathful and the meek, the successful and those who are failing — all of these do not require the same instruction and encouragement.
>
> If you look at it more closely, note how great a difference there is between those who are married and those who are not, and, among the unmarried, between those who live alone and those who live together in community; between those who are proficient and advanced in contemplation and those who barely manage to hold a straight course [in prayer]; and again, between city and country people, the simple and the clever, businesspeople and the leisured, those who have met with reverses and those who are prosperous and have known no misfortune.[21]

The people whom we mean to shepherd differ in countless ways, from natural qualities such as sex, age, and physical health, to environmental and social factors like marital status, affluence, knowledge, ethnicity, and occupation. The sheer diversity of human beings, even in a close-knit community, can be bewildering for those who aspire to guide them in

Christ. In one sense it is exciting to work with so many different kinds of people; yet, at the same time, it is perfectly understandable that pastoral leaders feel exasperated from time to time in the face of such diversity. How are we possibly supposed to lead toward the same God this many-headed monster that we call a Christian congregation? A middle-aged, lower-middle-class man with a working spouse and two children who has just been diagnosed with terminal cancer is obviously not in the same condition as an adolescent woman in good health, with supportive parents, plenty of resources, and a world of opportunities to look forward to. It is a challenge as old as the church. If we mean to bring the gospel to people where they really are, we must take account of their full particularity as best we can.

Yet Gregory notes that it is the differences between people's spiritual conditions that often distinguish them more than anything else — differences in temperament, psychological state, moral character, and the desires and appetites that make up our personalities. Ironically, it is often those who are extremely zealous in their piety who are the most difficult to lead, because they believe that they already know everything they need to know and have nothing else to learn.[22] Another common obstacle, which is in a sense the opposite of dogmatic zeal, is the sort of fickle eclecticism that accepts every teaching with equal truth and sincerity, holding on to nothing in particular. Eclectics can be just as difficult to guide as zealots, because whatever one may offer them will likely have no more effect than what they heard from the last person. A more obvious challenge is outright opposition that puts up explicit barriers and, in the worst cases, maliciously seeks to undermine the leader's good work and position of authority.[23] Interestingly, of all three groups, Gregory considers the self-righteous the hardest to lead — much as Jesus reserved his most venomous words for the Pharisees — because, psychologically speaking, active resistance to the gospel is much closer to faith than cold indifference or proud self-reliance.

Finally, and most importantly, there are the different stages of spiritual maturity in which we find people. As Paul writes, some Christians are spiritual infants who need the milk of elementary instruction, while others are more mature and require the solid food of advanced teaching (1 Cor. 3:1-2; see also Heb. 5:12-14). If the man with cancer mentioned above is spiritually mature with a deep experience of prayer and Christian living, and the adolescent woman is a brand-new believer with several habits that do not fit with the gospel, the situation will be turned yet again.

Providing the right level of teaching is extremely important for effective pastoral guidance, for, as with human infants, if we give new Christians food that is too advanced for them, it can be upsetting and even dangerous, causing them to lose the good growth they have already attained. Likewise, if we offer the more mature only introductory lessons, it will not be enough to sustain them, and they will easily become bored and angry at not being fed properly, and for that reason may lose their faith. Instead, we must give them God's hidden wisdom, which is suited to the spiritually mature (1 Cor. 2:6).[24] Since the ultimate focus of our work is on the soul, or the "inner person" of the heart (albeit existing in a deeply physical and social life), we should expect the key attributes and the chief problems we face to be those which are rooted in the mind and heart.[25] The ability to discern among the different conditions in which people find themselves is essential to good pastoral leadership.

Just as our people exist in many different conditions, so too there are different "treatments" that the competent pastor will apply to each case. Like a good physician, who has a range of medicines and therapies at her or his disposal, the skilled pastor must be acquainted with a full range of spiritual treatments that can be administered when needed.[26] Again, Gregory gives a representative list. Some need frank and direct instruction, while others are better taught by example. Certain people need to be encouraged, while others need to be actively restrained from what they are doing. The sluggish will need to be stirred up by being "smitten by the word," while the overzealous need to be cooled and restrained. Some need praise, others blame. Again, some people need to be rebuked publicly, but others should be approached privately. In some cases we should give direct and obvious attention, yet in others we should make people feel that they're being left alone (even though they really aren't). There are even situations where the good pastor must show anger or despair (without being overcome by them), whereas in others we must not be angry or despondent, or it would hurt the person terribly.[27] In order to be effective leaders, we must be able to provide whatever treatment is actually needed, adapting our ministry to the conditions of our flock.

Can anyone possibly perform such a complicated task? None of us is equally proficient at every sort of pastoral treatment. We tend to be naturally disposed to one set of approaches or another. Nevertheless, the people we serve will need them all at one time or another, and the church that is led by a one-trick pastor is a poor church indeed. One of the most common problems churches face is when a leader focusses excessively on one pastoral method. The pastor who understands herself mainly as an encourager of those who are downtrodden, to the point that she is constantly encouraging people in every circumstance, will inevitably be neglecting a whole segment of the flock which needs a different treatment. Or the pastor who knows how to lead only by proposing a strong agenda and forging ahead for all to follow will be at a loss when the situation calls for more gentle persuasion and patience. The same applies to preaching styles, approaches to one-on-one counsel, worship leadership, and administration. A given pastoral treatment — whether it be encouragement, exhortation, praise, or rebuke — is not going to be helpful in every situation, regardless of how good we may feel about offering it. To administer the wrong treatment in the wrong situation or at the wrong time can even be positively harmful.[28] As Gregory the Great warns, "often a wound is made worse by unskilled mending."[29]

To be sure, effective leaders make full use of their natural strengths and strong suits, but we must never assume that what we are best at is what people need. The medicine chest of a skilled leader must be full of different remedies, and what we lack we must make every effort to borrow, devise, or learn along the way. Here again the limitations of our personal preferences make themselves known, for we must be guided not by our own predilections, but by the needs of our flock. To rely on our favorite way of doing church is ultimately a form of pastoral selfishness. By contrast, true love of others calls us out of our comfort zones to provide the treatments that our people really need. For this reason it is important to have the flexibility to learn and adapt as we go. A good leader is always learning; we are constantly getting to know people and their situations, and we will always have weak sides to develop. The need to grow and change can be very challenging, but it is also what makes church leadership such an exciting undertaking. In the long run, the ability to learn and adapt is much more important than an immediate "fit" between leader and congregation in terms of favorite skills.

The art of pastoral leadership consists in a kind of well-informed spiritual adaptability. One must first be acquainted with the treasure chest of Christian theology and spirituality, knowing the full range of human attitudes toward God and the world. One must then diagnose the condition of each individual and group. And, finally, one must adapt oneself to the situation at hand, applying the appropriate treatment to each need, at the right time and pace. Gregory the Great writes, "spiritual directors should . . . carefully consider what things are suitable, for whom, when, and how."[30] Because human beings are "the craftiest and most complicated of creatures," a pastor must be like a skilled harp player, able to play many strings at a time, or an orchestral conductor who helps different instruments to join in making beautiful music together, as Gregory Nazianzen suggests.[31]

Pastoral leadership thus requires a diagnostic sense of both pathology and health, for in the Christian life they are always understood together. In this respect church leaders carry forward the ministry of Christ himself, who embodies both our sin and salvation, as the one who knowingly took on our condition and yet has the power to save and the desire to give us life and peace. The absence of one or the other can explain a lot about the extremes that sometimes substitute for real pastoral ministry, in which a given community is defined by either constant problems or naïve optimism.

Augustine gives a wonderful summary of these tasks in one of his sermons:

> The turbulent need to be corrected, the faint-hearted cheered up, the weak supported. The opponents of the gospel must be refuted, its insidious enemies guarded against. The impertinent should be instructed, the indolent stirred up, the argumentative checked. The proud should be put in their place, the desperate set on their feet, those engaged in quarrels reconciled. The needy have to be helped, the oppressed liberated, the good given your backing, the bad tolerated. And all must be loved. In all the vast and varied activity involved in fulfilling such manifold responsibilities, please give me your

help by both your prayers and your obedience. In this way I will find pleasure not so much in being in charge of you as in being of use to you.[32]

Note that, by sharing these instructions with his congregation, Augustine is communicating to them his vision for church leadership frankly and openly, just as Paul did with his communities. And like Paul he is teaching the entire community to care for itself in the same way (see 1 Thess. 5). Gregory the Great summarizes this shared work: "The speech of the teacher should be adapted to the character of his audience, so that it can address the specific needs of each individual and yet never shrink from the art of communal edification."[33]

Augustine gives two helpful examples in his work *On Catechizing the Uninstructed.* First, Christian teachers should try to find out the state of mind and the motives of those they teach, in order to adapt their teaching to the situation.[34] For example, with those who are highly educated and well read, one might first ask why they want to become a Christian and what they've read about Christ. One may then want to speak only briefly about matters that they've already read about, while at the same time stressing the authority of the scriptures and the great learning of Christian theologians of the past, who may be helpful in persuading the hearers of the truth of Christianity.[35] Yet with those who are especially eloquent or refined it may be important to stress that God approves those who avoid sin and evil more than those who merely avoid ugly speech or are concerned about matters of fine taste. And they should be taught that speaking well in church is a matter of faith and prayer more than worldly eloquence.[36]

The early theologians often called this diagnostic ability the gift of discernment. Both clerical and monastic teachers emphasize how important discernment is in order to grow in the Christian life, and especially for the work of spiritual guid-ance. Gregory the Great writes that a good leader must "apply discernment to distinguish between sin and virtue, . . . just as the nose discerns the difference between a sweet smell and a stench."[37] One of the accounts of discernment comes from the fifth-century monk John Cassian, who summarized much ear-lier teaching on the subject. John stresses first of all that the discernment of spirits is a gift of God, as Paul tells the Corin-thians (1 Cor. 12:10). He goes on to describe discernment as the kind of sure knowledge and good judgment that sheds light on everything that we do, like the sound eye, which is the lamp of the body (Matt. 6:22-23). Discernment is a kind of de-liberative thinking that guides our thoughts and actions as pastoral leaders. It is like the good sense and practical wisdom mentioned in Proverbs: "Where there is no guidance, a nation falls, but in abundance of counselors there is safety" (Prov. 11:14); or "Like a city with its walls down and no defense, such is the person who does anything without good sense" (Prov. 25:28). Discernment is the wisdom, intelligence, and judg-ment without which the spiritual life, like a house, cannot be built properly and supplied with every good treasure (Prov. 24:3-4). By enabling us to distinguish between good and evil (Heb. 5:14), discernment is "the mother, guide, and guardian of all the virtues," Cassian says.[38] Spiritual discernment even determines when the pastor should ignore one form of sin in order to conquer another that is more dangerous, such as per-mitting mild vainglory in order to conquer lust.[39] Benedict considered discernment the single most important quality in an abbot of a monastery.[40]

Church leaders of every age have warned of the danger of giving or receiving spiritual advice that is radically innova-tive, particularly on matters of great importance. John Cassian writes that discernment is given only to those who are humble, and in accordance with the tradition and the example of the ancients. It is not, therefore, to be equated with purely private judgment, for by definition the two are opposed (how can something be basic Christian teaching if no one has ever heard of it?).[41] If the direction we are giving does not accord with apostolic tradition as the church has publicly received it in diverse times and places, then it cannot properly be called Christian leadership. Augustine too writes, "If anyone tried to preach something different" from what the apostles teach, "such a person would be preaching his own ideas, not drawing from the central stream" of Christian truth. We should beware of trusting a pastor who seeks to guide us with his or her own original ideas. So Augustine concludes this particular sermon, "May this water, common everywhere to all, reflect the glory of God, not the private lives of human beings."[42]

One of the key aspects of pastoral discernment is that it helps us to avoid extremes in the Christian life, and in our spiritual direction.[43] Gregory the Great reminds us:

> We must skillfully balance things so that while we supervise with the virtue of humility, we do not relax just supervision. So let there be love that does not soften, vigor that does not exasperate, zeal that is not immoderate or uncontrolled, and kindness that spares but not more than is befitting.[44]

This principle of moderation frames the long section on the cure of souls in Gregory the Great's *Pastoral Rule,* which is organized in pairs of opposite conditions, such as rich versus poor, haughty versus meek, and so on. Ambrose gives equally helpful advice about the need for balance:

> Harshness and severity or excessive forgiveness are equally inappropriate. In the one case, it looks as if we

are wielding power tyrannically, and in the other as if we have taken on the responsibilities of an official position but are inept at discharging them.[45]

Consequently, Cassian says, the discerning pastor is well aware of the reality of God's grace in the Christian life and is wary of harsh or totalitarian measures in most cases.[46]

Conducting a multi-faceted, adaptive ministry does not mean that leaders are fickle or people-pleasers, but just the opposite. The adaptive spiritual *techne* that we have just outlined cannot be practiced by a leader who is diffuse, directionless, or without backbone. Paradoxically, it requires great stability of mind and heart to be able to practice this sort of adaptive ministry. Otherwise, we are not able to discern what congregants really need, but are randomly responding to one set of impressions after another. As Gregory Nazianzen puts it, the skilled pastor must be both "thoroughly simple in uprightness, and as far as possible multi-fold and varied in dealing with each individual."[47] Effective Christian leaders combine stability and flexibility, simplicity and multiplicity, in order to guide their flocks well.[48]

Well-rounded pastoral leadership will necessarily involve addressing the sins of our people, admonishing them to repent, hearing their confessions, and reconciling them when they are penitent. A ministry with no penitential element is drastically incomplete, and indeed it is positively cruel, because it leaves people in their most debilitating habits and conditions. Imagine how frustrating it would be to have a doctor who refuses to treat any real illness! Moreover, as Paul himself faced (see 1 Cor. 5; 2 Cor. 2),[49] there are certain kinds of flagrant and unrepentant sin that require the offenders to be excluded from the church, both for their own sake and for that of the community. Caring pastors will lament these situations, and will do everything in their power to avoid extreme measures. Ambrose puts the matter with great sensitivity:

> It is a distressing thing to have to amputate any part of the body, even if it is gangrenous, and it should be treated for a long time if it can be cured with any remedy. But if it cannot, then a good physician will cut it out. In the same way, it is the earnest desire of a good bishop always to heal members of the church body who are sick, to eliminate ulcers that are spreading, and to cauterize this or that part rather than cut it off. But, as a last resort, if a part cannot be cured, the bishop will cut it off — at great distress to himself.[50]

The subject of penitential discipline serves to remind us how crucial is the overarching relationship of love and trust for pastoral work. In a penitential situation, such a relationship makes all the difference between a mean-spirited put-down and loving guidance. Any leader who exhorts people to repent of their sins without having first established this relationship of love, trust, and care is committing an act of cruelty. In the marvelous words of Ambrose, "First and foremost, we need to realize that there is nothing more helpful than to be loved, and nothing more hurtful and devoid of benefit than not being loved." Church leaders must therefore take care to show "calmness of mind and liberality of heart above all, so that we may gain a place in people's affections."[51] Ambrose goes on to say that the love of people for their leaders even helps to attract newcomers, because when strangers perceive how much a leader is respected, it encourages them to place their confidence, and eventually their love, in the leader as well.[52] The way to inspire this love among one's flock, of course, is to follow the example of Jesus: we move our people to love us by loving them first (see

1 John 4:10-11), and we preserve love and trust by our ongoing generosity.[53]

This is one of the reasons why it is important for communities to have a direct role in the selection or approval of their leaders. For several centuries, in both the Eastern and the Western churches, Christian bishops were elected, or at least ratified, by their particular communities, and in most cases they came from the community originally. Where other processes of appointment are used, it is essential that ordained leaders receive the consent of the people, so that a pastoral relationship of love and trust can be established.

The cure of souls is not a foolproof method for manipulating people's spiritual lives according to a design of our own making. Nor should we imagine that by our heroic efforts we can produce a community of perfect people, uncontaminated from sin and evil. Such fantasies are often an escape from the hard work of loving others, and they appeal to human pride more than to the gospel of Jesus Christ. The Christian life is not about pretending that we can easily remove the residue of sin from ourselves or others; it is about constant repentance and a lifetime of receiving and administering God's healing grace, until God's final reign is one day established permanently.[54] John Cassian stresses that spiritual healing is a long-term project.[55] Focusing too exclusively on the ultimate result can at times impede our growth, as Abba Moses teaches Cassian.[56] Gregory the Great reminds us that pastoral guidance must be exercised in great humility by leaders who attend first of all to their own spiritual condition before God, "for the hand that would cleanse others must itself be cleansed, or it will soil everything that it touches." Those who hope to guide others must make sure that they continue to "prosecute the vices" in their own hearts and always direct others in fear and trembling at the great challenges that they face themselves.[57]

Over time the Apostle Paul came to be seen as a premier model of the adaptive cure of souls, beyond all other lawgivers, prophets, and apostles. Gregory Nazianzen collected a list of citations from Paul's letters to show how Paul's ministry was both simple and manifold, combining kindness and strictness at the appropriate time. Paul instructed both slaves and masters, rulers and ruled, husbands and wives, parents and children, the married and celibate. He addressed self-discipline and indulgence, wisdom and ignorance, circumcision and uncircumcision, Christ and the world, the flesh and the spirit. He administered different treatments at the appropriate time, accompanying, checking, excommunicating, grieving, rejoicing — and all for the cross of Christ and the best interest of his spiritual children.[58]

Yet, as Gregory himself confesses, to manage each of these types and conditions is not easy.[59] In the face of such a challenge, it is no wonder that leaders occasionally find it enticing to escape into more controllable activities. To lead people effectively requires much faith, grace, and priestly skill.[60] The cure of souls is not merely a specialized form of individual pastoral care, as it is often imagined (though of course it includes that). It characterizes the entire ministry of a pastoral leader, including preaching, Christian initiation, communal celebration, and penitential discipline. This overarching relationship of attentive spiritual direction provides the context and character of all our activities.

The Healing of Christ

The cure of souls that pastoral leaders administer is ultimately a participation in the ministry of Christ himself, as we noted in the first chapter. We are able to guide people toward God only to the extent that we abide in Christ and reflect

Christ's own guidance of us. In a real sense, adaptive spiritual guidance is itself what Christ *is* — it is the purpose of his becoming human in the first place. It was Christ, the eternal Son of God through whom the world was made (1 Cor. 8:6), who first adapted himself to our condition, in order to deliver us from sin and death and lead us back to God.

Augustine magnificently describes how Christ made himself to be the means of our growth and healing toward the unchangeably wise life that he from all eternity, so that he is both the way home and our home itself.[61] Because our lives are wrapped up in pride, the wisdom of God came to us in mortal flesh in order to save us through the folly of Christian preaching (1 Cor. 1:21).[62] Christ's incarnation is thus God's supreme healing treatment of us, "to restore sinners to complete health." Augustine describes how in Christ "Wisdom adapted her healing art to our wounds by taking on human existence, curing some of our ills by contraries and others by homeopathic treatment," just as a doctor does with physical ailments — only in this case Christ is both the physician and the medicine. When we had fallen through pride, Wisdom applied humility to cure us; when we were deceived by the craftiness of the serpent, Wisdom set us free by the foolishness of God, and cured our vices by the virtues of Christ. Homeopathically, Wisdom healed human beings by becoming human and defeating death by death. Such is the "Christian medicine chest" that Christ administers to us.[63] Indeed, it would be impossible for us to be purified and to know the eternal truth of God at all had Wisdom not adapted itself to our infirmity. Wisdom was made weak and seemed foolish by drawing near us, so that we might be able to draw near to God and thus to grow strong and wise.[64] Through faith Christ continues to guide us with "the medicine to heal the most corrupt customs" of human society.[65] In this sense the deep logic of pastoral therapy is really the doctrine of Christ himself, or orthodox Christology.

Scripture too "provides treatment for so many diseases of the human will," Augustine says. In the scriptures we are able to discover the will of God that has been adapted to our condition and conveyed to us through the human authors of the biblical books. The biblical writers in turn expressed their thoughts in the human languages of Hebrew and Greek, and these have since been translated into the many languages of the world for the salvation of the nations — all in a grand process of divine adaptation.[66] Likewise, the church's rule of faith and creeds as well as the eucharistic sacrament are medicine given to repair the sickness inherent in our minds and souls, Ambrose tells us.[67] It is to the resource of scripture that we turn next.

ology and the spiritual study of scripture lie at the heart of inspiring and effective pastoral leadership, and pastoral leadership is essentially biblical and theological. Week in and week out, the most practical thing that enables church leaders to minister well is our study of scripture and our theological rootedness.

Theology, or the knowledge of God and talk about God, is based in the reading and interpretation of scripture that takes place within the church's life of prayer and the practices of Christian discipleship. To some the idea of theologically centered leadership may seem impractical or even irrelevant. There are strong cultural forces and countless everyday pressures that, if not resisted, can keep our ministries from being theological at all. Yet centuries of Christian experience testify that where the church is truly thriving, a deep theological substance makes up the core of its life. People who are moved by God's grace are ultimately longing for words and practical gestures that will draw them more closely into the life of God. If they wanted anything else, whether food, money, political change, or emotional comfort alone, they would go to people who are more qualified to provide these things. But for spiritual and theological sustenance, they come to the church.

If we hope to have effective ministries, we must resist the idea that the more theological or spiritual one's ministry is, the less practical and relevant it is (and vice versa) — as if one could be concerned about, say, church budgets and care for the poor *or* the Bible and theology, but not both. Theology is not merely one subject among many; it is an inclusive and integrative project. As pastoral theologians have noted over the centuries, theology builds on and in a sense includes many other kinds of knowledge as the higher science into which they each fit and which gives them each their fullest meaning. Theology derives from scripture above all, whether studied directly or experienced in Christian worship, and it includes liturgy, church history, ethics, pastoral care — practically every subject under the sun, as Augustine stresses in *Christian Teaching:* "All good and true Christians should understand that truth, wherever they may find it, belongs to their Lord" and is "useful for the understanding of the holy scriptures."[2] The separation of theology from other arts and sciences and from the practical concerns of the church is one of the most regrettable developments of the modern period, and it undermines the Christian life.

Church leadership is theological by its very definition. When bishops and priests proclaim God's word and seek to lead people to love and worship God, they are participating in God's own dealings with the world. In his oration on the priesthood, Gregory Nazianzen writes that pastoral leaders administer the same healing grace and divine instruction that God has given to Israel and to the early church in the scriptures.[3] The biblical covenants not only establish the church and provide the content of its message, but in a real sense they include the present-day church and its leadership in a single continuum of divine grace. Well-functioning pastoral leadership is the direct intention of the law and the prophets and the "new mystery" of the incarnation and passion of Christ. Christian pastors administer the same loving-kindness and divine correction seen in scripture, which reaches back to the restoration of Adam and Eve.

Rooted in the interpretation of the Bible, theology is the lifeblood of the church and its ministries. In the scriptures Christians come to know Jesus Christ, the image of God the Father, as he is worshipped and obeyed in the teaching and the mysteries of the church, by the power of the Holy Spirit. Through the study of scripture we are also interpreting ourselves and the world in which we live. The knowledge and love of God revealed in the Bible is thus the cause, the blueprint, and the meaning of church leadership in every age.

Fortunately, most Christians have experienced theologically vital leadership in one form or another. Yet the pastoral literature of every age attests that there is always a need for theologically grounded leaders. Too often pastors feel that they have too little time and opportunity for prayer, study, theological development, and continuing education, and many regret that they didn't make more of their time in seminary or other formation programs to learn basic skills on which to build a lifetime of theological learning. Yet, if we are honest with ourselves, those of us who feel unavoidably busy are not devoid of our responsibility. There is more that we could do to make sure we are well grounded and fed. As Gregory the Great observes, people often "crave the opportunity to teach what they have not yet learned" and "appraise too lightly the burden of authority."[4] It is a great challenge to maintain a theologically centered ministry, yet it is extremely important all the same.

Here again we can draw encouragement from exemplary leaders of the early church who practiced the sort of theologically centered leadership that great pastors in every age have known. As we noted above, the primary job of church leaders is to shepherd God's people toward their heavenly life with Christ in the power of the Holy Spirit. We will be able to guide the baptized through their ongoing transformation in Christ only by being deeply rooted biblically and theologically.

The Resource of Scripture

All scripture is inspired by God and is useful for teaching, for reproof, for correction, and for training in righteousness, so that everyone who belongs to God may be proficient, equipped for every good work.

1 Timothy 3:16-17

The most immediate and practical means for maintaining a theologically centered leadership is holy scripture. It is through what the Apostle Paul calls the interpretation of scripture "according to the Spirit" that pastors are enabled to be effective guides. The centrality of scripture in the life of faithful church leaders can hardly be exaggerated. Unfortunately, people who have encountered some form of fundamentalism often imagine that the authority of scripture requires that all other forms of knowledge be considered false, whether they come from artistic expression, the humanities, or the physical, theoretical, and social sciences. In a fundamentalist mindset the matter is viewed in an all-or-nothing way, and different sorts of knowledge are seen to be mutually exclusive. But this is not the view of the early church and later catholic and evangelical traditions. For the great leaders of the Christian past holy scripture and the theological perspective it represents stand at the summit of human knowing, but not in a detached way — as if God's word were so weak that it could not relate to them without being destroyed! The opposite is also true: if one wants to give proper place for the human arts, it is not necessary to insist that they must compete with scripture for supreme authority.

Gregory Nazianzen and Augustine were among the most highly educated bishops in the early church, and they loved the Greek and Latin classics until their deaths. Yet each one praised the scriptures above all other literature as the pinnacle of human knowledge and understanding. Gregory calls the scriptures "the testimonies of God, to which I have entrusted my whole life,"[5] while Augustine writes that "the canon of scripture has been placed at the summit of authority for our salvation. By imitating its style a capable person will be influenced when he or she reads it."[6] And so, Augustine continues, bishops and priests are above all "interpreters and teachers of the divine scriptures."[7] The teaching of scripture is to be preferred even over people's wondrous experiences of God through dreams, visions, or miracles, for these are meant to lead us to the knowledge of God as he is revealed in the Bible.[8]

Consequently, the early theologians stress the importance of acquiring a solid theological foundation through biblical study in order to practice pastoral ministry. One must first study "the wisdom of God that is hidden in a mystery," Gregory says, and only then dare to speak about it to others.[9] Augustine likewise organizes his *Christian Teaching* on the same pattern, beginning with how to discover the meaning of scripture (books 1-3) followed by the communication of that meaning to others (book 4). Moreover, Gregory, Ambrose, and Augustine felt personally unworthy of pastoral office because they had not studied the scriptures sufficiently. Gregory and Augustine each arranged a period of retreat before beginning active ministry in order to undertake that study, while Ambrose remained frustrated that he was forced to learn while he was already teaching others. Gregory repeatedly states that one must first learn God's law, which the Spirit reveals to the good shepherd in the deeper meaning of the scriptures, and only then presume to teach it.[10] Gregory the Great adds that skilled spiritual guides can minister effectively only if they "meditate daily on the precepts of the sacred word, inspired by the Spirit of heavenly fear and love."[11]

Interpretation according to the Spirit

The main support for transformative ministry is what the tradition calls the spiritual interpretation of scripture. To read scripture "according to the Spirit" (2 Cor. 3:6) means to interpret it in Christ through the presence and work of the Holy Spirit. This takes place paradigmatically in the liturgy of the church, through the reading, hearing, prayerful response to, and sacramental celebration of God's word, as well as in individual and group study. It is important to remember that most Christians throughout history have not had private access to the written text of scripture. Normally they heard it read and preached in church, while some owned small collections of memorable passages, or possibly whole sections such as the Book of Psalms or Paul's letters. It was the clergy who had regular access to a complete copy of the scriptures owned by the local church, and it was their chief responsibility to study it and teach it to others.

There are many different ways that one can read the Bible. The very definition of the Bible itself already reflects interpretive choices being made. The Christian and Jewish ordering of the Hebrew scriptures, for example, are different, indicating their different perspectives on the meaning of the texts. The sort of biblical interpretation that inspires the life of the church and guides its leadership, however, is of a particular sort — even though, as we cautioned above, one that is incorporative rather than exclusive of multiple approaches. Spiritual interpretation stands against both fundamentalism and nihilism, as Augustine and many others have stressed. What we are focusing on here is a distinctively Christian way of reading the Bible, one that has been formed through the experience of actual church communities since the first century.

One way of defining the spiritual interpretation of Scripture is as that sort of reading that provides for transformation and growth in Christ by the power of the Spirit. It was this kind of reading that was discerned and practiced, with plenty of variation and idiosyncrasies, throughout the early church. It arises from the patterns of interpretation given in the New Testament itself, and it was discerned more systematically in the second and third centuries by theologians such as Irenaeus of Lyons, Tertullian, and Clement and Origen of Alexandria. Irenaeus is the first extant Christian writer who made use of all four gospels and most of the other New Testament documents, and who shows many of the basic patterns of reading that became standard in later generations. In particular, Irenaeus defines the sort of reading that corresponds with the church's "canon of truth" or "rule of faith." The rule of faith represents the belief that Christians confessed in baptism,[12] and it focuses on the incarnation, death, and resurrection of Christ within God's work of creation and final restoration. Through the rule of faith Irenaeus and other second- and third-century theologians witness to the church's single faith which holds across very different geographical and cultural contexts; and it helps to define the orthodox or catholic faith against major departures from it (schisms and heresies).

The greatest teacher of biblical interpretation and theology during this period was Origen of Alexandria. Origen influenced all of the major pastoral theologians we have been discussing, and much of Eastern and Western Christianity in general. Origen took special notice of key statements in the New Testament about the Bible, the Holy Spirit, and the knowledge of God. In 2 Corinthians 3 Paul writes that he is a minister of "a new covenant, not of the letter but of the Spirit, for the letter kills but the Spirit gives life." Speaking about the Old Testament scripture, he then argues that for those who are in Christ, the veil that lies over Moses is lifted and one can now see the divine glory conveyed through the scriptures. By seeing the glory of the Lord through the reading of scripture with the freedom that the Spirit brings, Christians are transformed more and more into Christ, who is the image of God and the one through whom God is known.

In his previous letter to the Corinthians, Paul also wrote that "God has revealed these things to us through the Spirit, for the Spirit searches everything, even the depths of God," and that he speaks "in words not taught by human wisdom but taught by the Spirit, comparing spiritual things with spiritual" (1 Cor. 2:10, 13). In these and other passages,[13] Paul makes it clear that only by the Holy Spirit, in Christ, can one understand the truth of scripture and know the "deep things" of God.[14] Equally important for early biblical interpretation is the story of Jesus' meeting the disciples on the road to Emmaus. On the way, Jesus opened the scriptures to them in a new way, "interpret[ing] to them the things about himself in all the scriptures" (Luke 24:27).

Christian spiritual interpretation moves from the more obvious, literal sense of the text to its deeper meaning — what Origen called the "spiritual gospel."[15] What makes the scriptures holy or divine is not so much the words themselves as the teachings they convey (although the words are necessary to convey that meaning). Through the pages of scripture the Holy Spirit seeks to reveal those teachings that are needed for the growth of the church and individual souls. These include above all the knowledge of God, the identity and work of Christ in relation to both God and humanity, and the Holy Spirit, through whom God is known, as well as the life of the church.[16] In other words, the chief revelation of scripture concerns the Trinity: Father, Son, and Holy Spirit. These are the three main topics or "articles" found in the early rules of faith and in the formal creeds of the later church councils, and this Trinitarian structure is reflected in the works of theologians such as Origen, Gregory Nazianzen, and Augustine.[17] Through the Bible the Spirit communicates what the tradition calls "saving doctrine" — salvation meaning not only Christ's justification of sinners through his death on the cross and the basic faith of Christians, but our full growth and perfection in Christ that will be revealed at the Last Judgment.

Augustine gives a helpful summary of spiritual interpretation:

One is able to speak more or less wisely to the extent that one has made progress in the holy scriptures. I don't mean just reading them frequently and committing them to memory, but understanding them well and diligently exploring their senses, . . . to see into the heart of them with the eyes of the heart.[18]

The progress that one makes through the study of scripture cannot be measured by how much one reads or even knows by heart, because it is not the words themselves that ultimately matter, but how deeply one perceives their meaning in the core of one's being. As Origen observes, the aim of Christian biblical interpretation is not merely to learn what the text literally says, nor even to master the history of Israel and the early church. The Bible is not primarily a historical record of God's people or a collection of literary works with various aesthetic qualities (though it certainly is both of these). Rather, the primary purpose of the scriptures is to convert and transform the church and individual souls to the knowledge and love of God. When the fathers speak of the scriptures as being divinely inspired, it has to do mainly with the spiritual transformation that the Spirit produces when they are read, rather than with any particular theory of verbal inspiration (which is more the concern of modern fundamentalists). The divinity of the scriptures is shown first of all through their power to change lives, against the contrary forces of the world and the powers of evil.[19]

This means that the spiritual interpretation of the Bible is very much about power, just as church leadership itself is. It is no accident that Origen's first proof of the divinity of scripture is the conversion and faith of Christians, and especially the divine power displayed in martyrdom (which Origen's own father suffered), together with the general success of the apostolic mission, despite its humble beginnings and the brevity of

Jesus' teaching compared with the sages of Greek antiquity. Paul himself writes, "My speech and my proclamation were not with plausible words of wisdom, but with a demonstration of the Spirit and of power, so that your faith might rest not on human wisdom but on the power of God" (1 Cor. 2:4-5). When we speak of biblical interpretation for ministry, we are talking about a life-changing experience.

Christian truth reaches far beyond mere literal accuracy or historical fact; it is larger than historical or literal truth, even though our knowledge of it depends on coming to grips with the literal meaning of the text. Paul speaks in terms of different sorts of nourishment. Those who are of the flesh can receive only milk; one must be spiritual in order to take solid food (1 Cor. 3:1-3). Again in the Letter to the Hebrews, the basic elements of the scriptures are milk, whereas solid food is more advanced teaching of the word of righteousness, which only "those whose faculties have been trained by practice to distinguish good from evil" can receive (Heb. 5:12-14).[20] To grow in Christ, one must move beyond the basic sense of the text in order to perceive its deeper meaning, which applies both to the depth of the human heart and to the future life of the community of believers. It therefore poses a major obstacle to interpretation if one takes a merely intellectual or aesthetic approach to the text, with no personal engagement beyond that. Yet the opposite problem can be equally pernicious: namely, a fundamentalism that enforces a deadening and often heretical literalism, coupled with a fierce intolerance of all who disagree.

Bringing together a number of biblical texts, Gregory Nazianzen asks passionately whether aspiring church leaders have really undergone this transforming study of scripture:

Whose heart has never been made to burn as the scriptures were opened to him (Luke 21:32) with the pure words of God that have been tried in a furnace (Psalm

12:7)? Who has not attained the mind of Christ (1 Cor. 2:16) by a triple inscription of them on the breadth of his heart (Psalm 22:20 LXX), or been admitted to the treasures that remain hidden to most people, secret and dark, and made to gaze on the riches within (Isa. 45:3), and so to become able to enrich others, comparing spiritual things with spiritual things (1 Cor. 2:13)?[21]

This sort of biblical study necessarily involves the moral transformation and spiritual growth of readers as they come to share more and more in the life of Christ. What we normally think of as moral growth is often the most reliable gauge of spiritual growth, even though Christian righteousness cannot take place apart from the grace of Christ and it always leads to what are ultimately spiritual ends. Preachers like Origen and John Chrysostom, for example, often focus on the mundane ways of Christian living in light of the spiritual truths that they have proclaimed from scripture. The aim of spiritual interpretation is actually to participate or share in the things that one learns — to go beyond merely hearing or understanding them in order to *live* them.

Augustine analyzes the process of growth involved in spiritual interpretation. First we begin with the fear of God, as the Psalmist says (Psalm 111:10),[22] facing our mortality and allowing our flesh and our pride to be nailed to the cross of Christ. With this fear we acquire a humble and modest piety that is prepared to believe the truth of scripture. Fearing God and believing the truth of scripture, we then come to the divine knowledge that God wants to impart to us. The knowledge that we are meant to love God with all of our being then moves us to mourn over our various idolatries and to seek God's further help. When our love of the Trinity is perfected we come at last to the stable enjoyment of God's Wisdom, which is Christ himself.[23]

Paul gives various indications of the difference between literal and spiritual meanings. A key statement comes in Romans 2:28-29:

> A person is not a Jew who is one outwardly, nor is true circumcision the one that is in the flesh; but a person is a Jew who is one inwardly, and true circumcision is of the heart — it is spiritual, not literal.[24]

Both Paul and the Letter to the Hebrews also distinguish between the earthly and the heavenly Jerusalem (Gal. 4:25-26; Heb. 12:22).[25] Similarly, Paul speaks of "Israel according to the flesh" (1 Cor. 10:18) — which, given his other statements that "it is not the children of the flesh that are children of God" (Rom. 9:8) and "not all Israelites truly belong to Israel" (Rom. 9:6), implies that there is also an Israel according to the Spirit. In light of these passages, the Christian reader can see that when the scriptures speak of Israel, Jerusalem, or the covenant of circumcision, they refer in a deeper sense to the *spiritual* Israel and the *heavenly* Jerusalem, which is the church as it grows to maturity in Christ, beginning now and culminating in the age to come. Spiritual exegesis means that the literal meanings and events in scripture are applied to Christ, the church, and the growth of the individual soul toward God. As Paul writes elsewhere, the words of the law and the prophets were written "entirely for our sake" (1 Cor. 9:10).[26]

For the great early theologians the spiritual meanings of scripture are virtually endless and cannot be categorically defined in any neat system. As working pastors know, it is important not to get bogged down in technical hermeneutics, except when necessary for the clarification of matters that are unclear or for the defense of basic Christian beliefs. Among the spiritual senses of scripture are instances of figurative language; typology (for example, Paul's statement that the rock in the wilderness of the Exodus was Christ, 1 Cor. 10:4); allegory (Hagar and Sarah as an allegory for the two covenants, or the earthly and heavenly Jerusalem, Gal. 4:22-26); and Christological (the figure of Wisdom in Prov. 8; the Suffering Servant of Isa. 53), ecclesial, and eschatological meanings. The broad category of typology includes references among the Old and New Testaments to the final consummation between earthly and heavenly realities, and between the temporal scheme narrated in scripture and the eternity of God's heavenly kingdom. Yet there is one division of meaning that orthodox theologians vehemently resist, and it is important for us to register it here, especially given the history of anti-Semitism. The church fathers do not regard the Old Testament itself as the letter that kills and the New Testament as the spirit that gives life, as if the literal history and scriptures of Israel were corrupt. Theologians of the second and third centuries spent great energy defending the truth and inspiration of the Old Testament scriptures and their unity with the New Testament. Rather, both Testaments contain literal and spiritual meanings, and even the New Testament provides only a shadow of things to come.

The literal sense of the scripture is basic to the entire enterprise of Christian interpretation. While the spiritual senses transcend the literal sense, it is the literal meaning of the text that gives rise to the spiritual, and which remains the necessary basis of all spiritual interpretation. Without the literal sense, there is no spiritual sense. Contrary to what some have assumed over the years, spiritual interpretation does not threaten or eliminate the literal meaning of the Bible. Here again it is important to avoid the sort of envious thinking that insists that an idea can be valid only if it excludes all other meanings. The spiritual meaning of scripture is not the contradiction of the literal sense, but its fuller meaning and disclosure. Just as human infants cannot skip over the need to feed on mother's milk and go straight to solid food, so too a good reader of scripture never skips over the literal meaning in order to arrive at a spiritual understanding. To do so would be distinctly unspiritual. Christian spiritual interpretation, like other kinds of theological-cultural reading, makes the literal meaning *more,* not less, important, by making it present and relevant here and now in the life of the church. We should also note that there are some passages — direct moral instruction being the most obvious example — where the literal and spiritual meanings are so close as to be almost the same thing.

Hence, while the authors of scripture were limited human beings, and the various biblical books were produced in concrete and complicated historical situations, it is *through* (not in spite of) these all-too-human, earthly means that scripture conveys the knowledge and love of God to us. In this sense the scriptures are like "treasure in earthen vessels" (2 Cor. 4:7), as Paul uses to describe his own bodily fragility.[27] Even in antiquity some people were reluctant to accept the human qualities of the Bible or believed that they should be able to know God directly, without any mediation, assistance, or the labor of study. Augustine argues strongly against such views, pointing out that all knowledge of God is mediated in one way or another, and he gives notable examples of this from the scriptures themselves.[28] In scripture divine knowledge comes to us through conventional linguistic signs uttered in real historical situations. The Bible is thus a complex mixture of literal or historical meaning and spiritual truth,[29] just as Christ himself is a mixture of humanity and divinity in order to serve as a mediator between God and human beings. Historical contingency and human authorship are not obstacles to divine meaning any more than Jesus' humanity is an obstacle to our knowledge of God through him; in both cases the human and the earthly are the very means through which the divine is communicated to us. The goal of biblical interpretation is to mas-

divine meaning often shines through most clearly, precisely because the literal difficulties present such a sharp contrast. Origen and Augustine both suggest that these difficulties are designed by God and placed in the text in order to help our understanding. Whether in puzzling passages or in the general hiddenness of divine meaning, God deliberately conceals deeper truths from those who are not prepared to receive them, out of compassion for the needs of their growth. And yet, at the same time, God's larger purpose is to *reveal* divine truth to us, even through the difficulties and concealment of scripture. Augustine writes that God intends to open to his people the obscurities of scripture and

> the shadowy depths of the mysteries hidden in them, so that they may freely feed there. "And in his temple each one cries out 'Glory!'" for in his church every one born again to an eternal hope praises God for the gift that he or she has received from the Holy Spirit.[32]

The most reliable practice for understanding difficult passages is to interpret them in light of other ones that are clearer. This is one of the ways in which the rule of faith functions in biblical interpretation, to provide basic ideas by which one can understand more ambiguous ones. Origen referred to this sort of comparative interpretation with Paul's phrase "comparing spiritual things with spiritual" (1 Cor. 2:13),[33] and Augustine similarly insists on giving priority to clear, central texts.[34]

Like milk and solid food, both simple, literal meanings and deep, spiritual ones have their place in the larger process of biblical interpretation and spiritual growth. Augustine notes the rightful place of both senses in a beautiful description which compares the relatively simple rhetorical style of the scriptures with more ornate classical literature:

You see how accessible to everyone is the very style in which scripture is composed, even though very few can enter deeply into it. Like a close friend, it speaks without pretense the clear ideas that it contains to the heart of the unlearned and of the learned. It does not exalt the things that it conceals in mysteries with a proud language to which the sluggish and uneducated mind dares not approach, as a poor man dares not approach a rich one, but invites all people with its lowly language. And it not only feeds them with evident truth but also exercises them with hidden truth, though it has the same truth in clear matters as in hidden ones. But so that obvious truths do not become repugnant, the same truths are again desired as concealed, and as desired are in a sense refreshed, and as refreshed they are taught with sweetness. By these, evil minds are helpfully corrected, little minds are fed, and great minds are delighted. That mind is an enemy to this teaching that either, because it is in error, does not know that it is most salutary or hates its medicine because it is ill.[35]

Scripture is accessible to all, even as it constantly seeks to draw us more fully into its depths.

The literal and spiritual meanings of scripture all point ultimately to Christ, in the fullest sense: the eternal Son of God who has become flesh for our salvation, who even now has a body on earth, which is his church, and who one day will come again in glory to bring about the fulfillment of all things according to God's plan. Augustine writes that in Christ God's divine Wisdom has adapted itself to our condition as both the way and the destination, both the physician and the medicine, and both the sign and the signified of scripture.[36] As we noted above, when Christ is being referred to in a spiritual way, such references do not replace or contradict the basic historical or literal meaning of the text, as if one could have *either* historical *or* Christological meanings. The apostles and the great theologians of Christian tradition recognized that we always have both. Augustine writes, "In the scriptures we come to know Christ; in the scriptures we come to know the church."[37] As the ultimate meaning of scripture, Christ is both the life of the church and the model of the love of God and neighbor.[38] When Christians read scripture by the work of the Holy Spirit, they come to have "the mind of Christ" (1 Cor. 2:16) — to know, to worship, and to love Christ, and to love God and neighbor as Christ does. When we study scripture frequently, carefully, and deeply, by the inspiration of the Spirit, we receive the living water that Christ gives, and the mind of Christ is formed in us.[39]

The scriptures' ultimate reference to Christ always points us forward to the future and final state of the church, compared to which our present knowledge and love of God are incomplete. In this sense the meaning of scripture constantly leads us onward to the spiritual growth that we have yet to attain. Origen emphasizes that we can never understand all of scripture, and so we must constantly strive to grow further in Christ, to "reach out both to better works and also to a clearer understanding and knowledge, through Jesus Christ our Savior,"[40] in the same way that Paul "presses on toward the goal for the prize of the heavenly call of God in Christ Jesus" (Phil. 3:14). Augustine too stresses that we will never attain the direct vision of God in this life, and so the signs of scripture are given to us for a lifelong process of discovery. Even the incarnation of Christ is but a shadow of things to come, as Peter, James, and John were shown on the Mount of Transfiguration (Mark 9:2-8).

The sort of knowledge that scripture yields is not merely information about past events and God's will in the present. Instead, through these things the Bible brings us into direct contact with God, as the Holy Spirit comes to dwell within us and gives the knowledge of God the Father through his Son Jesus Christ.[41] Augustine argues more clearly than perhaps anyone before or since that the ultimate purpose of scripture is that we come to know Christ in such a way that we truly love God and our neighbor — that God is to be loved purely for God's own sake and our neighbor is to be loved also for God's sake.[42] This summary is deceptively simple on the face of it, but it is extremely difficult to grasp, not only because we are weak in understanding, but because our loves are confused and disordered. It takes more than a lifetime of spiritual training to learn to love God and our neighbor fully. As we come to understand more and more the deeper truths of scripture, Augustine says, our faith will eventually become vision, hope will become bliss, and love will become even more love.[43]

The spiritual interpretation of scripture through study, prayer, preaching, and teaching is the immediate source of the pastor's work. It is also the best protection against a rigorist approach to pastoral holiness and our efforts to turn Christian spirituality into a program of self-help or works righteousness. Church leaders do not maintain a spirit of holiness by undertaking a self-motivated program of moral improvement; they grow in Christ by dwelling regularly in the spiritual depths of scripture. This is not because the standard of holiness is any lower than we imagine it to be, but because the power of God to sanctify and empower pastoral leaders through their study of scripture is much greater than we believe. Without the personal transformation that comes from spiritual interpretation, pastoral leadership is "the gravest of dangers" and "of all things most to be feared," Gregory Nazianzen warns.[44] It is a crass exercise of human power to attempt to guide others when one has not been guided oneself by the healing Word and Spirit of God. Yet the positive side is even truer, and should inspire us with great confidence: in the scriptures God has graciously provided the means by which church leaders are empowered by the Spirit to share in Christ's own redemption of the world. Only the spiritual study of scripture can produce the theological mind and heart that make church leaders effective in the eyes of God and of God's people.

As a fitting summary, Gregory Nazianzen gives a moving description of this sort of biblical training in his memorial oration for his late friend Basil.

> Who more than [Basil] cleansed himself by the Spirit and prepared himself to be worthy to discuss divine things? Who was more enlightened by the light of knowledge and penetrated into the depths of the Spirit and with God beheld the things of God? . . . To search all things, even the deep things of God, is witnessed by the Spirit (1 Cor. 2:10) — not because the Spirit is ignorant of them, but because it delights in the contemplation of them. Now all the things of the Spirit had been investigated by Basil, and from them he instructed us in every aspect of character, taught us the loftiness of expression, deterred us from things present, and refashioned us toward things to come.[45]

Pastoral Theology

Nothing is so magnificent to God as pure doctrine and a soul that is perfected in the dogmas of the truth.

Gregory Nazianzen

To return to where we began, church leadership is theological in its origin, definition, method, and ultimate aims. Pastoral ministry is a direct extension of the grace that God has conferred since the initial covenant with Abraham. The spiritual reading of the Bible is also preeminently a theological enterprise. The baptismal confessions contained in the early rule of faith and the later conciliar creeds are a kind of summary of scripture, focused on the passion of Christ, and also a guide for reading it in a Christian way.

The most striking thing about these early statements of faith is that they are focused on and structured around the Holy Trinity: God the Father, Christ the Son of God, and the Holy Spirit, who is equally divine with the Father and the Son. Since apostolic times, theologians have argued that the substance and shape of pastoral ministry, like the life of the church itself, is expressed above all in the doctrine of the Trinity. Through baptismal confessions, the exposition of scripture in the eucharistic liturgy, doctrinal disputations, poetry, hymnody, and numerous Christian practices the early church proclaimed its faith in the Trinity as the heart of its meaning and mission — what Gregory Nazianzen summarizes very simply as "the worship of Father and Son and Holy Spirit, the one Divinity and power in the three."[46]

Among the many subjects that church leaders must teach, the most important of all, Gregory says, is the doctrine of the Trinity.[47] There are some subjects of Christian teaching that we can expect will change over time with advances in humanistic and scientific knowledge, such as the nature of the cosmos and the natural world, human psychology, and angelic and demonic influences. Yet there are also certain essentials of the faith that remain fundamentally the same over time and in diverse contexts, such as the fact that God created the universe, the truth of the Old and New Testaments, the incarnation, passion, death, resurrection, and second coming of Christ, the final judgment, "and above all what pertains to the supreme and blessed Trinity." In his work *Christian Teaching* Augustine too writes that the only thing that is to be loved and enjoyed purely for its own sake and able to make us happy for eternity — and hence the one and only thing that the scriptures serve to reveal to us — are "the Father and the Son and the Holy Spirit, the Trinity . . . which is shared in common by all who enjoy it."[48]

Despite many popular ideas about it, the doctrine of the Trinity is not a mathematical puzzle of how three things can be one, or an abstract idea about God. It is the confession of God's presence and saving work through the biblical covenants and in the current life of the church. For centuries the church has proclaimed its faith in God the Father Almighty, creator of heaven and earth; in Jesus Christ, the only Son of God, who was begotten of God the Father before all worlds, was crucified and rose from the dead for us, and will come again to judge the living and the dead; and in the Holy Spirit, who proceeds from God the Father before creation and is the Lord and giver of life — and that the Son and the Spirit are each fully divine, possessing the divinity of God the Father while remaining distinct from the Father and each other. "Theology," in the most basic sense of the word, means to know and confess the sovereign God who created the universe, and that the Son and the Holy Spirit, who have been met in the covenants recorded in scripture, are also God. More generally, theology means to speak about God or for God in multiple ways on the basis of this Trinitarian confession.

Gregory Nazianzen was given the title "the Theologian" in Eastern Christian tradition on account of his preeminent teaching on the Trinity. In his fifth *Theological Oration,* he gives one of the most succinct and illuminating summaries of the Trinity in all of Christian tradition:

> "There was the true light, which enlightens everyone who comes into the world" (John 1:9)[49] — the Father.

"There was the true light, which enlightens everyone who comes into the world" — the Son. "There was the true light, which enlightens everyone who comes into the world" — the other Paraclete (John 14:16, 26). "Was" and "was" and "was," but one thing was; "light" and "light" and "light," but one light and one God. This is what David too imagined long ago when he said, "In your light we shall see light" (Psalm 35.10 [36.9]). And now we have both seen and proclaimed the concise and simple theology of the Trinity: out of light (the Father) we comprehend light (the Son) in light (the Spirit).[50]

In the most basic and far-reaching sense, Christian theology is the knowledge of the divinity of God the Father in the person of Jesus Christ, the divine Son of God, by means of the inspiration of the Holy Spirit, who is also divine. In this way, Gregory concludes, Christians come to know God (Christ) from God (the Father) in God (the Holy Spirit), and by faith we are incorporated into the same knowledge and love that the Trinity has within itself.[51]

By dwelling in the spiritual meaning of scripture within the life of the church, Christians come to share in God's own life and being through Christ and the Holy Spirit, which is the purpose for which we were created and the ultimate goal of our existence. Christian theology, then, as summarized in the doctrine of the Trinity, is ultimately about participating in God's life, and in this sense it is virtually synonymous with what traditional theologians call divine illumination, contemplation, and the vision of God. Because we are finite and sinful creatures, we can never hope to fully understand the infinite, all-powerful, and holy God. But by God's grace, mercy, and love towards us, we are able truly to know God, even if only partially, in the face of Jesus Christ by the inspiration of the Holy Spirit, until we finally come to see God face to face.

This lived, participatory knowledge of the Trinity is the content, the structure, and the ultimate aim of the Christian life, and it involves everything that we encounter in scripture and come to know about the world and human life. Gregory tells his congregation how they are to live with the theology of the Trinity: "You have grasped something; now pray to grasp the rest. Love what abides within you, and let the rest await you in the treasury above."[52]

Sound theology is so central to the work of church leadership that it is a necessary part of pastoral ministry. As Gregory argues, what makes one a bishop with "the true right of succession" is not merely rightful ordination or the external credentials of office, but the truth of one's faith and doctrine — that one believes and teaches "in an apostolic and spiritual manner."[53] The crucial importance of orthodox teaching is a factor that runs throughout early Christian literature, from Ignatius of Antioch in the early second century[54] to Augustine in the fifth century. As Gregory notes, it is the chief mark of a faithful bishop to "cultivate the whole world with the fair seeds and doctrines of piety."[55] Gregory praises his associate Basil the Great for "revealing to us the Holy Trinity" through all of his practical and didactic forms of ministry. Basil shows "unshakeable faith and sincere loyalty to the Trinity," which is "the only true devotion and saving doctrine."[56] Looking back on his own ministry at the Church of the Resurrection in Constantinople, Gregory reminisces, "I watered this parched flock with my words and sowed the faith that is rooted in God."[57] Such is the goal of exemplary Christian leaders in every age.

Contemplation in Action

The centrality of biblical interpretation and theology explains why healthy and effective pastoral leadership is rooted in a lifetime of study and learning, for which pre-ordination training is at most a thorough introduction. John Chrysostom puts it succinctly: good preaching comes not from raw talent or pure inspiration, but through arduous study. While a good preacher surrenders to the prompting of the Holy Spirit when delivering a sermon, Chrysostom says, he or she will spend a substantial amount of time studying the scriptures and other sources in preparation to preach.[58] We must be unflinchingly honest with ourselves here: no amount of professing that we want to entrust our ministry to God, or claims of divine inspiration, can take the place of serious and focused theological study. Augustine insists that to imagine that one can understand Christian truth on one's own, with only oneself, the Bible, and God, as it were, is a dangerous example of pride, since one presumes that one doesn't need the guidance of other wise interpreters.[59] It is self-deception, not to mention a theological error, to think that our efforts in study somehow conflict with the inspiration of the Holy Spirit.[60] On the contrary, God works through the pastor's study and prayer, just as he works through the effort of all Christians to read and understand the Bible.

Contrary to the prevailing culture of busyness, disciplined study and prayer are not a distraction or escape from more important "practical" matters of ministry; they are the most practical activities of all. Theological study is exactly the sort of activity that seems unimportant and not urgent, but which in fact is extremely important and holds enormous potential for benefiting our work in the long run. Regular study and prayer must therefore be planned, scheduled, and protected from the more urgent but less important interruptions that arise (granting that some interruptions are truly important). The witness of many church leaders shows that the disciplined study of scripture and classic Christian sources, together with a regular and deep prayer life, will make our ministries surprisingly strong and effective. Prayerful spiritual interpretation and sound Christian theology, in communion with authoritative interpreters of the Christian past, makes for great preaching and sensitive listening, and wise words of counsel, and it serves to empower all the baptized in their own ministries for Christ's kingdom.

The great pastoral theologians of the early church are unanimous in their insistence on the importance of spiritual study for church leadership. As we have already observed, both Gregory Nazianzen and Augustine, when they were ordained, took an extended time to prepare by studying the scriptures in depth, and they didn't believe they were qualified for the office until they had done so. Gregory writes of Basil that "before he was a priest, he trained himself in the divine words." For his part, Ambrose lamented that, because he was snatched directly from civic administration into the priesthood, he had to begin teaching others before he had learned much himself, so he was forced to learn and teach at the same time.[61] He is therefore honest and straightforward about the time and care that the pursuit of divine wisdom requires.[62] Jerome too advises his friend Nepotian, "Read the divine scriptures constantly; indeed never let the sacred volume be out of your hand. Learn what you have to teach."[63]

When it is done properly, church leadership is a balance of activity (which includes preaching and counseling) and contemplative study and prayer. For most clergy it is a great challenge to maintain a dependable pattern of study and prayer. Gregory the Great, who had himself been a city administrator before entering the clergy, knew all too well how the many tasks of active ministry can divide the heart and mind of church leaders.[64] He writes soberly, "No exhortation can encourage the laity, no reproof can correct their sins if the person who is supposed to be a protector of souls becomes the executor of earthly affairs." Gregory's insight here is shrewd:

external activity can be exhausting in a way that we perversely enjoy because it gives us a sense that we're doing something important, even while we grow ignorant of God in our hearts. When a pastor has become preoccupied with busywork, Gregory says, the shepherd has simply abandoned his flock.[65]

The aim of church leaders should be to balance active ministry and compassion for our neighbors with prayer and a life of study and contemplation, so that our hearts dwell constantly with God and at the same time are mindful of the needs of others. "Inwardly one considers the hidden things of God; externally, one carries the burdens of fleshly people," just as Jesus and Paul did.[66] In order to do this we must constantly put spiritual matters first, meditating daily on the sacred word,[67] for the health of the entire community.

Chrysostom, Augustine, and Gregory the Great each ministered in a full sacramental context. They stressed the importance of baptism as the beginning of the Christian life, and
their worship each week centered on the Holy Eucharist and
was supported by regular prayers of various sorts. Yet they all
believed, without exception, that the main focus of pastoral
work and the heart of church leadership is not "ritual activity"
per se, but the administration of God's word through preaching, teaching, and pastoral counsel within the celebration of
the mysteries of the church. As Gregory Nazianzen puts it,
"The first of all our concerns is the distribution of the word."[1]

This may seem surprising to those who are accustomed to
defining the priesthood chiefly in terms of eucharistic celebration. Yet it need not be. In the early church, the sacraments are not understood as being divided from the ministry
of the word, in the way that became common in certain later
understandings of "word and sacrament." First of all, the sacraments — or in Greek, the "mysteries" — of the church include many types of services, such as the celebration of
Easter, observances of the martyrs, and a whole variety of religious festivals and prayer services, in addition to practices
such as singing spiritual songs or marking oneself with the
sign of the cross.[2] Secondly, with regard to baptism and the
Eucharist, which Gregory calls "the mystery of divinization"
in a special sense,[3] the sacrament is the entire worship service, including the biblical readings and sermon, not merely
what happens at the baptismal font or the eucharistic table;
and these parts centrally involve the use of words anyway,
mostly drawn from scripture and earlier traditions of prayer.
In *Christian Teaching* Augustine defines a sacrament as a reve-
latory sign of any kind, including certain material things, and
the premier example of a sacrament is the scriptures and the
events and institutions reported in them.[4] The priest's work
of biblical exposition and preaching is thus an integral part of

the sacrament, from the standpoint of the major patristic theologians. For Gregory biblical interpretation itself is a sacrament, as are the names of God, Christ, and the Holy Spirit.[5] It is in this broader sense of sacramental practice, rooted in the language of scripture, that church leaders have been given the authority to forgive sins (John 20:23) and to offer salvation from God, as John Chrysostom says.[6]

In the mind of the early church, it is misleading to think of word versus sacrament. Even Augustine, who tends to speak of them as parallel terms, focuses to a surprising degree on the effective ministry of the word. In patristic literature there is no sense that sacramental acts will take care of themselves, as it were, regardless of the quality of preaching and pastoral counsel. Such a view would be considered anathema to any bishop or priest worth his salt — and this is so, we might add, in every period of church history. Without exception, the church fathers consider the power of the spoken word, especially in the sermon, to be an essential and irreducible component of effective pastoral ministry.

This focus on the ministry of the word can be seen in a sermon that Augustine delivered for the celebration of Saints Peter and Paul:

> This reading of the holy gospel (John 21:15-19), which sounded in our ears just now, is very apt for today's feast — if it descended from our ears into our hearts, and there found a place of repose. God's word, you see, reposes in us, when we find rest in the word of God. Then it admonishes all of us who minister to you the Lord's word and sacrament to "feed his sheep."[7]

God's word is at the heart of the feast, and Christ expects pastoral leaders to feed his flock with the word, so that they can fill the hearts of all the faithful. In another sermon, Augustine speaks of God's word in terms that we usually associate with eucharistic communion: "When I expound the holy scriptures to you, it's as though I were breaking bread to you. For your part, receive it hungrily, and belch out a fat praise from your hearts."[8] At the center of pastoral ministry, then, is the feeding of God's flock with the word that fills and moves the heart and leads us to praise God.

Christian Doctrine

Pastoral leaders are primarily interpreters of the scriptures, as Augustine notes, teaching Christian truth and opposing falsehood and error.[9] In order to understand the scriptures and the Christian faith, people need a wise teacher and "the recommendation of our forebears."[10] Athanasius gives similar advice to the abbots and bishops he supervised in the Egyptian desert. To the monastic leader Ammoun he writes, "Strengthen the flocks under you, father. Encourage them with the apostolic writings; lead them with the Gospels; counsel them with the Psalms."[11] Athanasius tells a certain Draconitus, who was reluctant to take up the pastoral office,

> The laity expect you to bring them food, which means the teaching of the scriptures. They expect to be fed — but remain hungry because you feed only yourself. When our Lord Jesus Christ comes and we stand before him, what excuse will you give when he sees that his own sheep were starved for nourishment?[12]

How often are people starving for nourishment, either because they lack pastoral teaching or because they do not know Christ at all? Human life itself, Augustine says, is like the desert mentioned by the psalmist (Psalm 62:3), where "our souls are parched and our flesh thirsts in countless ways." Many people simply long for a tolerable way through the desert. Without guidance in how to find God, who is the ultimate object of our longing, we are left to wander through the "pitiless, horrible and terrifying" land that is human life. Of course, it is the conviction of the church that we are not hopeless wanderers, but people who have been redeemed by Jesus and whom he wants to lead home to himself. Augustine explains:

> God has taken pity on us and given us a way in the desert, our Lord Jesus Christ, who is himself the way (John 14:6). And that is not all — he has provided strengthening companionship for us in the desert by sending us preachers of his word. And he has given us water in the desert, filling his preachers with the Holy Spirit, to be in them a spring of water leaping up to eternal life (John 4:14).[13]

By God's grace the ministry of Christian preachers rescues people from the desolation that we all eventually must face. It is therefore incumbent on church leaders to focus their energies on nourishing the laity with the food of God's word in scripture, for their very lives are at stake. In another sermon Augustine comments on Psalm 71:3:

> Those who are preeminent in the church by their radiant holiness are mountains because they are fit to teach others. They speak in such a way that other people can be soundly instructed, and live in a way that others can safely imitate.[14]

Above all else, the teaching of the scriptures in a spirit of holiness is the premier task of the leadership of the church.

When he began his own priestly ministry, Gregory Nazianzen told his congregation that Christ had given them a pastor who would guide them by his teaching, and whose words the Spirit would engrave deeply in their hearts, "not with ink, but with grace."[15] Like Augustine, Gregory was convinced that "the leaders and teachers of the people, who bestow the Spirit," have as their main task to "pour forth the word of salvation from their high thrones."[16] Without this nourishing and saving ministry, one is not really leading God's people, but merely taking up space that should properly be filled by someone who is committed to being a real pastor. In all he or she does, Gregory says, the priest is a steward, or administrator *(oikonomos)*, of God's word, sharing in God's economy *(oikonomia)* of salvation that began in the covenants.[17] Gregory portrays his ministerial ideal in the way he describes his late friend Basil:

> His beauty was virtue. His greatness was theology. His course was the perpetual motion that carries him by ascents even to God. And his power was the dissemination and distribution of the word.[18]

This all sounds very inspiring in theory, but to administer God's word effectively is a difficult work indeed. Augustine admits the difficulty of his burden with courage and frankness:

> The gospel terrifies me, because no one could outdo me in enjoying such anxiety-free leisure. There is nothing better, nothing sweeter, than to search through the divine treasure chest [of scripture] with nobody making a commotion; it's pleasant, it's good. But to preach, to refute, to rebuke, to build up, to manage for everybody — that's a great burden, a great weight, a great labor. Who wouldn't run away from such a task?[19]

And yet, Augustine admits, it is far worse *not* to preach the word: "Do you see how dangerous it is [for us bishops] to keep silent? . . . It is our business not to keep quiet, and it's your business, even if we do keep quiet, to listen to the words of the Shepherd from the holy scriptures."[20] Gregory the Great too cautions against a naïve belief that Christian teaching is easy:

> Spiritual guides must be careful not only to guard against saying something wrong, but also to avoid offering the right words too frequently or unprofessionally. The virtue of what is said is often lost when it is enfeebled in the hearts of the audience because the speech was offered hastily or carelessly.[21]

Gregory continues,

> Whoever undertakes the priesthood assumes the office of a herald, so that wherever he goes he proclaims the coming of the dread Judge. Therefore, if the priest does not know how to preach, with what voice will such a mute herald proclaim?[22]

Our job as leaders is challenging not only because life is hard and people are starved for God's word. Church leaders also face considerable opposition to the task of feeding people with the word of God. We do not live in a desert that is an arid, neutral space; we live in a world that positively seeks to mislead us with lies and falsehood. The purveyors of falsehood are many; they are skilled at what they do and are often well funded and established. Augustine therefore asks with urgency: when the wiles of falsehood are so clever, how can Christian preachers allow themselves to "state their truths in a manner too boring to listen to, too obscure to understand, and too repellent to believe?" How can any responsible pastor abide that those who sell lies are able to "terrify their hearers by their style, move them to tears, make them laugh, and give them rousing encouragement, while those who speak on behalf of truth stumble along slow, cold, and half asleep?" When the arguments for falsehood are so compelling and well crafted, the advocates of the truth need all the skill they can muster in order to defend the truth, to refute error, and to speak well and persuasively.[23] Christian truth needs as many "weapons in the hands of its defenders" as we can provide.[24]

In his work *Christian Teaching* Augustine has given probably the most helpful definition of good Christian preaching that we possess. He adapts a passage from the Roman orator Cicero to provide a simple but powerful rule for good preaching:

> An eloquent man once said — and what he said was true — that to be eloquent you should speak so as to teach, to delight, and to sway. Then he added, teaching your audience is a matter of necessity, delighting them a matter of being agreeable, but swaying them a matter of victory.[25]

Three functions of good preaching, with three different aims. Preachers teach in the hopes of being understood; they delight their hearers with the manner of their delivery in order to be heard and enjoyed willingly; and they ultimately aim to sway them in order to cause them to obey God's word.[26] Note that each function has a clear and tangible goal. Good Christian preaching is always results-oriented. Augustine gives another helpful summary:

> The interpreter and teacher of the divine scriptures, the defender of right faith and the hammer of error, has the duty of both teaching what is good and unteaching what is bad. And in this task of speaking it is his or her duty to

win over the hostile, to stir up the slack, to point out to the ignorant what is at stake and what they ought to be looking for.[27]

Such results take concentration and labor to achieve, and they are not easy to come by.

Teach

The first and most basic aim of Christian preaching is to teach something. After all, people cannot believe in, hope for, or love what they do not know.[28] The immediate aim of teaching, of course, is to be understood. "There's no point in speaking at all if people don't understand us!" Augustine warns.[29] Pastoral leaders must first of all speak in order to be understood — not merely to express what we intend (to "speak our minds"), still less to show how clever or learned we are, but actually to convey the truth of Jesus Christ to others in a way that they can hear and receive. A good preacher orients everything he or she does toward this fundamental goal, eliminating from the sermon anything that gets in the way of being clearly and effectively understood, including unfamiliar technical terms. Especially when people listen to us quietly and are unable to ask questions when they need to, we must work hard to make sure they can understand what we are trying to get across.[30]

For this reason the most important single quality of good preaching is clarity of thought and diction. We must speak clearly and intelligibly because everything else depends on people's understanding what we are trying to say. It is impossible to cure souls and move people toward God if we are not communicating clearly what people need to hear. As every good preacher knows, we must also teach the basics of the faith over and over again because most people spend their entire lives coming to learn them. "The preacher should realize that he should not draw the souls of his listeners beyond their strength, otherwise the cord of the mind, so to speak, will be stretched too tightly and will break," Gregory the Great cautions.[31] And our teaching must always be that of Jesus Christ, as we noted in chapter one. Augustine writes,

> Christ himself will help me to say true things, as long as I don't just say my own thing. If I do just say my own thing, I will be a shepherd feeding myself, not the sheep. But if what I say is Christ's thing, then it is he who is feeding you, whoever may be speaking.[32]

Every serious church leader recognizes how crucial it is to be understood, regardless of how we feel about what we've said or how we said it.[33]

The Pastoral Epistles and several other New Testament texts are quite earnest about the necessity of good and faithful teaching. Paul writes to Timothy, "Until I arrive, give attention to the public reading of scripture, to exhorting, to teaching"; and later,

> I solemnly urge you to proclaim the message; be persistent whether the time is favorable or unfavorable; convince, rebuke, and encourage, with the utmost patience in teaching . . . rightly explaining the word of truth. (1 Tim. 3:13; 2 Tim. 4:2; 2:15)

A bishop must have "a firm grasp of the word that is trustworthy in accordance with the teaching, so that he may be able both to preach with sound doctrine and to refute those who contradict it" (Tit. 1:9). Good and faithful teaching is so central to effective leadership that a preacher who is technically eloquent but teaches falsehood is more to be pitied than anyone, Augustine says.[34]

A memorable illustration of faithful teaching is Gregory Nazianzen's portrait of Basil standing up to the Roman imperial authorities, who were urging him to profess ideas that he believed were dangerously false. Though he was threatened with severe punishment Basil replied that, no matter what the emperor demanded, he would not renounce his faith in the divine Son of God. At this, the official boiled over with rage and threatened Basil with the imperial wrath, but Basil showed that he had no fear of such measures. The official then exclaimed in amazement, "No one has ever spoken to me in this way and with such boldness," to which Basil simply replied, "Then perhaps you have never met a bishop!" Such was his commitment to Christian truth and the responsibilities of his office. Basil went on to explain that bishops are exceedingly gentle and modest people — except when it comes to defending the things of God, in which case they are bold and fearless of any worldly authority.[35] Gregory adds that Basil would have willingly suffered expulsion from his see and even exile and death in order to defend right teaching, or "orthodoxy."[36] Would that every pastor had such steadfast dedication and commitment to the gospel!

John Chrysostom writes that "the way of right teaching is narrow and hemmed in by threatening crags on either side."[37] When a priest is incapable or unwilling to use the scriptures to combat false teaching, it can cause people to doubt what they formerly believed and to cease to trust those whom they formerly relied on. Consequently, "a great storm descends on their souls, that this mischief results in a total shipwreck."[38] One of the best indications of whether we have taught our flocks effectively — whether they have understood what we have communicated — is that they are then able to teach others. Paul directs Timothy, "Be strong in the grace that is in Christ Jesus, and what you have heard from me through many witnesses entrust to faithful people who will be able to teach others as well" (2 Tim. 2:1-2).

The work of teaching mainly has to do with what we say; everything else is how we say it. There are some people who are eager to listen to a clear sermon and will do their very best to apply its message in their lives. For them a simple, didactic sermon is enough; if we provide good, clear teaching, their lives will be truly changed, and nothing more is needed.[39] And then there are all the rest!

Delight

Most people need more than clear, unadorned teaching in order to receive the spiritual food they need. The second function of Christian preaching is to delight our hearers. When we preach, it is important to do so in a way that is pleasing to hear, so that our people will pay attention and want to hear us. Delighting involves anything that is not strictly the substance or message of what we're saying, or an attempt to move people to action. It can be a clever turn of phrase, our choice of words, the sound of our voice, or a bit of humor to lighten things up. Augustine compares delighting speech to the spices that most people need in order to take in even the most necessary food.[40] For anyone who is not already prepared to listen to us through thick and thin — which is normally most of our hearers — we need to include such elements in order to be effective preachers.

Speaking in a pleasing way is especially important when we are covering familiar territory. Whenever we teach things that people have heard before (which is much of the time), if we speak in a flat, didactic fashion, we are almost certain to bore them and drive them away from our purpose. We must therefore take extra care to speak in a way that holds people's attention.[41] Similarly, it is important to modulate the style and intensity of our speech. It is annoying to listen to someone who constantly speaks in the same tone, whether calm, moderate, or intensely grand. Our preaching should alternate among these different styles, according to the needs of the moment.

The pleasing quality of our preaching has a single and clear purpose, which can easily be missed. The only purpose of delightful speech is to keep people's attention and to make them want to hear what we're saying. If we're not careful, the aesthetic qualities of a sermon can distract people rather than lead them more deeply into the word. We should never tell a joke or make a witty pun simply to entertain people, let alone to show them how clever and funny we are. If someone goes away from the sermon remembering the anecdote or the joke more than they remember the message of the scriptures, we have failed of our purpose.

Ambrose gives an excellent description of the appropriate use of delight:

> Preaching too should not always take exactly the same form, whether it be about the doctrine of faith, the teaching of self-control, the discussion of issues having to do with justice, or encouraging people to be diligent in what they are doing. Rather, as the scripture reading suggests itself, we should take it up and follow through as far as we can. Our exposition should not be excessively drawn out, but nor should it be broken off too soon: it ought to leave behind neither a sense of distaste nor an impression of carelessness and inattention. Our language should be pure, simple, clear, and plain, full of seriousness and dignity. It should not be studied with el-

egance, though it should also not lack a touch of appeal. . . . We need to beware of jokes even when telling stories, in case they distract people from grasping the more serious and profound point we're trying to make. . . . And concerning the voice, all that matters is that it is plain and clear. . . . The aim is not to affect a theatrical cadence but to keep a pace that is appropriate for speaking of the mysteries.[42]

Pleasing speech is necessary for good preaching, but its purpose is only to make Christ known and obeyed. In any case, it is more important to speak truthfully than to speak pleasingly. If anyone is unable to speak with both truth and delight, Augustine cautions, "let him say wisely what he does not say eloquently, rather than say eloquently what he says unwisely."[43]

Sway

If clear teaching is the most basic element of good preaching, the ultimate goal is to sway our hearers with the word of truth. Even the truest and clearest teaching is futile if we do not bring people closer to God. Only by actually moving our hearers to new levels of faith, hope, and love — by motivating their hearts, minds, and wills to new commitments and actions — have we accomplished our purpose as church leaders. Anything less falls short of the mark. Swaying is therefore the real victory of the preacher. Our hearers' full, active assent to the truth of the gospel is the only thing that really matters in the end, and it is our sole object.[44] As Paul writes to the Galatians, "The only thing that matters is faith that works through love" (Gal. 5:6).

We are ultimately trying to persuade people to *do* something, to love God and their neighbors more fully, not merely to understand our ideas or appreciate the style of our delivery.

Truly eloquent preachers are those who can sway their hearers by the force of their words.[45] Unlike the secular state, which moves people by force, Christian preachers move them by the persuasiveness and conviction of their words, John Chrysostom says.[46] Augustine gives a moving description of what this looks like, in a passage that deserves to be framed and displayed in the study of every preacher:

> Just as our hearers are delighted if you speak agreeably, in the same way they are swayed if they love what you promise them, fear what you threaten them with, hate what you find fault with, embrace what you commend, deplore what you strongly insist is deplorable; if they rejoice over what you say is a cause for gladness, feel intense pity for those whom your words present to their very eyes as objects of pity, shun those whom you proclaim in terrifying tones are to be avoided; and anything else that can be done by eloquence in the grand manner to move the souls of the listeners — not merely to know what is to be done, but to *do* what they already know is to be done.[47]

Love, fear, hate, embrace, deplore, rejoice, pity, shun — each one a revolutionary verb. We are talking about profoundly active *results.* If our preaching is effective, people's desires, affections, thoughts, judgments, and commitments will be drastically changed. A good preacher aims for nothing less.

Augustine reports from his own experience that he knew when he had preached a successful sermon. It was not by any applause he received, but by the tears that his people shed.[48] The applause that we often seek shows only that people are being well instructed. But tears show that they are being swayed,[49] whether they be tears of remorse, tears of repentance, tears of joy, or tears of gratitude. As we discussed in chapter two, we should be wary of praise and displays of approval because our aim is not to please people but to change their lives. It is impossible to do this by clear and pleasing speech alone. Again, Augustine writes,

> If our listeners are to be moved rather than merely instructed, so as not to become sluggish in doing what they know they should, and to give a real assent to the things they admit are true, more forceful kinds of speaking are called for. Here what is necessary are words that implore, rebuke, stir, check, and whatever other styles help to move the minds and spirits of our audience.[50]

As we teach the different texts and subjects of scripture, we should always keep in mind the aim of our teaching, which is "love from a pure heart and a good conscience and unfeigned faith" (1 Tim. 1:5).[51] By keeping this goal always before us, we direct everything we say to the purpose of causing our listeners to believe, and by believing to hope, and by hoping to love.[52] Even many people who know what they ought to believe and do still do not follow through. Therefore we must learn to be adept at all of the modes of exhortation and persuasion: encouraging, rebuking, admonishing, praising, imploring, checking.

Preaching is thus a preeminent instance of the cure of souls. As we stressed in chapter three, we must know how to administer each of these saving remedies in the right situation and in due season in order to be effective preachers. Augustine tells his own people,

> My dear brothers and sisters, your love has heard in the holy scriptures how bishops are placed in great danger, if they are unwilling to carry out what the apostle urges on them: "Preach the word, keep at it in season, out of season; admonish, rebuke, exhort with all patience and

positive instruction" (2 Tim. 4:2). And because such a heavy weight hangs over our necks, seeing that we are told, "If you do not declare to the wicked man his wickedness, I will require his blood at your hand" (Ezek. 3:18), we are obliged to take to task, either privately or publicly, those of careless life.[53]

Church leaders are charged by God with the admonition and exhortation of Christ's flock through all manner of persuasion. Moving speech is not an option in good preaching, nor a superficial adornment, like a nice flourish to round off a sermon. It is what God requires of us most of all. Not to rebuke someone who needs it is to be unfaithful to God and cruel to our neighbor, who depends on our help in this way.

This is serious work indeed, and it should now be clear why a new Christian is in no position to accomplish it. A church leader who refuses to take such an authoritative position with his or her flock is an imposter. On the contrary, a faithful and courageous pastor cares enough to say, "Son, as you undertake the service of God, stand in justice and fear, and prepare your soul for temptation" (Sir. 2.1), Augustine notes. Only the pastor who is prepared to speak like that will be able to strengthen the feeble and make them sturdy, to lift them off the sand and place them on the rock that is Christ.[54] Of course, it is possible to speak delightfully and movingly about things that are false, so our efforts to sway our hearers must always be founded on the truth.[55]

Such things are admittedly hard to judge. Whenever we have a sense of regret that we could have said something better than we did, it is important to remember that our people's impressions of what we have said often differ greatly from how we think things went. Since our goal is changed lives, we must rely not on our own feelings in the matter, but on our hearers' response.[56] The real effect of our preaching is usually not what people tell us immediately after the service; it is what their behavior shows weeks or months later. Our aim is to change lives, and such results usually take time and discernment to perceive.

In order to teach, delight, and sway people, we need, finally, to vary our style among calm, moderate, and grand speech, both to keep our listeners' attention and to apply the style appropriate to each subject, alternating like the waves of the sea.[57] A good preacher knows that the intense, grand style should be used only briefly, or it will lose its effect; whereas a plain conversational or didactic style can be heard for much longer.[58] Yet the style of our speech has more to do with deep feeling than fancy language. Our choice of words "should follow the ardor of the breast," Augustine says — it should be natural, rather than excessively planned and orchestrated,[59] and it should be guided by the substance of what we say. In good Christian preaching substance always drives form. It is the substance of what we say — the message of God's justice and mercy — that we aim to teach, delight, and sway people with, for even the command to love cannot be properly understood if the things to be loved are not true.[60]

Study and Prayer

The principles of good preaching are more about the heart than a matter of perfect rhetorical technique. High levels of education and specialized rhetorical training, such as Augustine and Gregory Nazianzen enjoyed, are certainly valuable in church leadership if one uses them well. Yet all the fathers insist that whatever training and education one has, what really enables one to teach, delight, and sway others in Christ is a prayerful faith, founded on the spiritual study of scripture. Church leaders should study and learn as much as they can —

the more the better, all other things being equal. But what makes it all edifying for our flocks is the faithfulness of our prayer and the degree to which the Holy Spirit moves in our hearts and gives us to speak the words of God.[61] The real school of Christian rhetoric is to read the scriptures and listen to effective preachers, just as infants learn to speak by imitating adult speakers.[62] The most important preparation for good preaching, Augustine reminds us, is "the progress that one has made in the holy scriptures."[63]

Augustine beautifully describes the relationship between God and human preachers in a sermon he delivered on Psalm 76. Commenting on verse 4, "Glorious are you, more majestic than the everlasting mountains" (NRSV), he notes that it is God who sends the light that comes from the mountains, which are the preachers of truth. The first such mountains were the apostles, "intercepting the first glimmers of your rising light." Yet Augustine stresses that it is not the mountains that illumine us:

> There have been plenty of people who imagined that the mountains themselves were the source of the illumination they received, and so they formed factions and raised up their own mountains; but then the mountains collapsed and they were crushed. . . . How can they think that their salvation is to be found in human beings, not in God?

So Augustine tells all believers, clergy included,

> Listen, everyone, the light comes to you through the mountains, certainly, but it is God who illumines you, not the mountains. . . . Is it the mountains that you trust? . . . Are you stuck there in the mountains? . . . There is something greater than the mountains!

While Christians rightly "lift our eyes to the mountains" (Psalm 121:3), the next phrase of the Psalm tells us the ultimate source: "My help comes from the Lord, who made heaven and earth." So, Augustine concludes, "To the mountains I have indeed lifted my eyes, because it was through the mountains that the scriptures were shown to me; but I have set my heart on God, who sheds light on all mountains."[64]

We are faced with a paradox: God is the source of all our ministry, and yet there is much that we must do in order to be true mountains through which God's light will shine. Here we must remember Augustine's stern warnings against fundamentalism. Any preacher who believes that the Holy Spirit will speak through him without any labor on his part is only making excuses for his laziness or fear, or else he has fallen into the error of believing that our efforts somehow get in the way of God's Spirit. Instead, God works through our own efforts and hard work, Augustine maintains. Just as physical healing comes from God through the use of medicines and the doctor's art, so God works through human teaching to produce spiritual growth.[65]

In a sermon on Psalm 119, Augustine says that

God teaches from within, but faith comes through hearing. And how will people hear without a preacher (Rom. 10:14, 17)? God gives the increase, unquestionably, but that does not mean there is no need for planting and watering (1 Cor. 3:6).[66]

Elsewhere he comments,

We speak because the Lord has graciously imparted to us the same Spirit who inspired those who spoke before us, and whatever we say now we say under the influence of the same Spirit who prompted our predecessors. We cannot omit to say it, therefore; it must be said, since it has always been said through the gift of God.[67]

The main way that the Spirit inspires us to speak, week in and week out, is through our study of scripture and our diligent efforts to teach and preach persuasively. On Psalm 67:13, Augustine warns,

> The Lord will give his word to [preachers] and enable them to preach the gospel, but only if they "sleep in the midst of their allotted inheritance." That is, only if they are careful not to desert the authority of the two Testaments will the word of truth be given to them. If they hold to it, they are the silver wings of the dove, and by their preaching the church is gloriously borne up to heaven.[68]

The prayerful study of scripture and our manner of life are of the utmost importance if people are going to listen to us and obey what we say.[69] And people will be much more likely to hear what we're saying if they can tell that we enjoy preaching and teaching![70]

The Leader

The business of Christian preaching is a mysterious mixture of divine and human affairs. One of Augustine's favorite metaphors for preachers is the rain clouds that figure regularly in the Bible. All who speak God's truth, from the prophets and apostles to the preachers of the church, and indeed all Christians, are like the clouds in Psalm 56. They are mortal creatures living in the flesh, yet also people from whom "the Lord flashes the lightning of his miracles and thunders his commandments." Even though preachers are mortal and fallible beings, "there is light concealed within them, just as the clouds have an inner luminosity from which they produce lightning."[71] It is from these very clouds that God's "lightning has flashed around the earth" (Psalm 96:4). The clouds appear dark until the lightning flashes, just as God's preachers can even be despised by the world, as the apostles were, "until something that amazes you leaps out from them."[72]

As one such cloud himself, Augustine is keen to admit both his desire to preach well and also his own limitations: "Would that the Lord my God would graciously number me among his many clouds — though let him see what a dense cloud I am!"[73] Despite their weaknesses, the clouds speak with confidence and joy in the God who is above and beyond them. Preachers are both heavens (in Psalm 89) because of "the blazing glory of truth" that they proclaim, but also clouds because of their mortal flesh. Whatever the heavens preach is from God and about God, Augustine says: "That is why they preach without misgivings, for they know to whom they are preaching, and they know that over him whom they preach they will never have occasion to blush." When we bear in mind that "no one among the clouds is God's equal" (Psalm 89:6), we have confidence to preach of God in spite of our frailties and limitations.[74] "They are exalted not by their own strength but by God's grace; but for their own part and in their own estimation they are valleys that humbly gush with springs."[75]

One of the most reliable marks of good church leaders is their willingness to confess their own weakness and God's glory. At the end of his great work *Christian Teaching*, Augustine says that he has laid out

> not what sort of pastor I am myself, lacking many of the necessary qualities as I do, but what sort the pastor

should be who is eager to toil away, not only for his own sake but for others, in the teaching of sound — that is, Christian — doctrine.[76]

Augustine tells his congregation, "I am bold enough to exhort you, but at the same time I boldly take a look at myself. After all, it's a futile preacher who speaks God's word outwardly, who isn't also listening to it inwardly."[77] In another sermon he says,

> Let us administer reproof, certainly — but first of all to ourselves. You wish to reprove your neighbor, and nothing is a nearer neighbor to you than yourself. Why go far away? You have yourself right there in front of you.[78]

Throughout our ministries, we must first draw near to God, so that we ourselves are the first object of our teaching, delighting, and swaying.

Gregory the Great concludes his *Pastoral Rule* with a similar admonition to reflect humbly on our own condition before the God who empowers us to serve him. Especially after we have ministered effectively, we must consciously examine and humble ourselves to prevent vainglory: "A consideration of one's weakness should subdue one's every achievement so that the swell of pride not abolish one's good works before the eyes of the secret judge."[79] For the faithful pastor the work of preaching and teaching is never ending, because Christian growth is an ongoing process. Augustine writes,

> Just as the reading of God's word has to be repeated every day, to prevent the vices of the world and thorns from taking root in your hearts and choking the seed that has been sown there (Matt. 13), so too the preaching of God's word has to be repeated to you always, or you may say you haven't heard what I say I have said.[80]

The work of preaching by the "heavens" that proclaim God's glory (Psalms 18:2; 19:1) aims at making all believers into such heavens. "You too can be a heaven if you wish," Augustine tells his hearers. "Do you want to be a heaven? Then purify your heart of earth and 'seek the things above where Christ is'" (Col. 3:1-2), and "mean what you say when you respond that your heart is 'lifted up'" at the beginning of the eucharistic canon.[81] The aim of all our work, after all, is to build up the entire body of Christ.

> We clergy instruct you with sermons; it is up to you to make progress in your conduct. We scatter the seed of the word; it is up to you to produce the crop of faith. Let us all run the course in the paths of the Lord, according to the vocation with which we have been called by him. And may none of us look back (Luke 9:62).[82]

Notes

I

1. For this reason Augustine called them "three letters of the apostle that anyone charged with the role of teacher in the church ought to keep before his or her eyes." *Christian Teaching* 4.16.33.

2. The categories of prophets and teachers (Acts 11:27; 13:1-3; 15:32; 21:9; Rom. 12:6-7; 1 Cor. 12:28) seem to be itinerant, like the apostles, while also being similar in some ways to local elders and overseers, which makes it difficult to ascertain the exact nature of their identity and work. In any event, the New Testament and other second-century texts show a strong concern that itinerant prophets be tested and subject to the authority of local leaders (see, e.g., Matt. 7:15; 1 Cor. 12:3; 1 John 4:1).

3. Including earlier works such as Philippians, the intermediate Acts of the Apostles, and the later Pastoral Epistles.

4. 1 Cor. 12:28: administration is a spiritual task in the church. Leadership (*kubernesis*) here is presumably more mundane (teaching is listed as 'higher'). See also 1 Tim. 3:14-16. Acts 14:23: Paul and Barnabas "appointed elders in each church"; see also Tit. 1:5. In 1 Tim. 3:1, the bishop is now singular; deacons are listed next, then presbyters after 5:17. It is interesting that there are no known textual variants in the manuscript tradition that make the plural "bishops" in Phil. 1:1 singular.

5. *Oration* 2.3.

6. *Oration* 2.16, 111.

7. PG 46.581.

8. Augustine, *Sermon* 46.30.

9. Augustine, *Sermon* 126.3. Here Augustine is playing on the fact that as a bishop he stood on an elevated platform in the liturgy, which he takes to be a symbol of his overall pastoral supervision. Note that in Augustine's Bible the numbering of the Psalms is at times one off from that of our modern Bibles. Based on the Old Latin version, Augustine's numbering corresponds with that of the Septuagint (LXX).

10. E.g., Gregory Nazianzen and John Chrysostom both refer to bishops and presbyters with the same term, priest/priesthood *(hiereus, hierosunes)*.

11. See also Mark 3:16; 6:7; Matt. 10:1.

12. *To the Ephesians* 2.2. See also *Didache* 15: do not despise [bishops and deacons]; 1 Clement 40.5.

13. See esp. *Oration* 1.6; 2.3-4, 16, 78; 9.3-4; 12.2; 13.4. For Gregory's terms cited here, see *Oration* 2.4: spiritual leadership *(hegemonia)* and service *(leitourgia)*; 2.78: authority *(prostasia)* and governance *(epistatein)*; 2.111: presidency *(proedria)*.

14. *On the Priesthood* 3.6.

15. Augustine's punning Latin is difficult to capture in English: *Praepositi sumus, et servi sumus. Praesumus, sed si prosumus! Sermon* 340a.3.

16. Augustine, *Sermon* 340a.1, 2. See also *Exposition on Psalm* 103(3).10: "the preachers of the word are laboring oxen (1 Cor. 9:9-10) and your servants."

17. *Pastoral Rule* 2.6.

18. *Sermon* 359f (Dolbeau 2).10.

19. *Oration* 2.3; see also 16.3.

20. *Sermon* 340.1. See also *Sermon* 339.1; 340a.8.

21. *Duties of Leaders* 1.205, citing his friend Lawrence.

22. Lit. "Demonstrate your bravery in your son."

23. *Duties of Leaders* 2.122.

24. *Sermon* 340a.4, 6.

25. In Augustine, see also *Sermon* 46.1. In Gregory the Great, *Pastoral Rule* 1.8.

26. *Exposition on Psalm* 96.10. See also *Sermon* 296.13.

27. *Sermon* 340a.9. See also *Sermon* 46.2; 296.13.

28. See, for example, Gregory the Great, *Pastoral Rule* 1.10, as late as the sixth century.

29. Gregory Nazianzen, *Oration* 2.114; a point on which Gregory the Great agrees entirely, *Pastoral Rule* 1.7.

30. The phrase appears throughout Paul's letters. In John, see 6:56; 14:23; 15:4-11; 17:21-23, 26; see also 1 John 2:6, 24-28; 3:6, 9, 15-17, 24; 4:13-16; 5:20; 1 Pet. 3:16; 5:10, 14.

31. Sarah #2, in *Sayings of the Desert Fathers: The Alphabetical Collection,* ed. Benedicta Ward. London: Mowbrays, 1975.

32. *Sermon* 46.30. On Christ as the one true shepherd, see also Gregory Nazianzen, *Oration* 18.4.

33. *Sermon* 339.4.

34. *Sermon* 134.1.

35. *Oration* 2.23-26; see also 16.13.

36. Gregory Nazianzen, *Oration* 2; John Chrysostom, *On the Priesthood* 1.6; 2.2; 3.7, 12, 17; Ambrose, *Duties of Leaders* 1.4 [II] (119); Gregory the Great, *Pastoral Rule,* introductory letter; see also 1.6-7.

37. *Sermon* 355.2.

38. See 1 Cor. 3:10-15; 4:5; also Rom. 14:12; Heb. 4:13; 1 Pet. 1:17. Augustine, *Sermon* 383.1. See also *Sermon* 17.2.

39. *Sermon* 296.3-5.

40. Rom. 15:30; Col. 4:31; 1 Thess. 5:25; 2 Thess. 3:1. Augustine, *Sermon* 340.4.

41. *Pastoral Rule,* Introductory Letter; 1.7 (27).

42. See Augustine, *Sermon* 46.30; 137.4.

43. *Didaskalia Apostolorum* 2.33, trans. R. H. Connolly (Oxford, 1929).

44. *Oration* 2.22; see also 9.3.

II

1. *Letter* 13.

2. *Pastoral Rule* 1.10.

3. *akolouthia pneumatike. Oration* 6.1.

4. *Oration* 2.50; 43.26.

5. *Oration* 9.2; 19.2.

6. *Oration* 6.9.

7. *Oration* 12.1; 2.39.

8. *Oration* 6.1-2; 7.3; 8.5; 15.13; 20.1-4; 39.14; *Carm.* 2.1.12.475-574. See also Gregory the Great, *Pastoral Rule* 2.2.

9. *Oration* 2.3.

10. *logos poimantikes, Oration* 2.34.

11. *Oration* 32.12-13.

12. Syncletica #12, in *Sayings of the Desert Fathers.*

13. *Pastoral Rule* 2.5.

14. *Letter* 13.

15. *Duties of Leaders* 2.41 (2.VIII); 2.60 (2.XII). Trans. Davidson adapt.

16. *Exposition on Psalm* 126.3.

17. *Pastoral Rule* 1.10.

18. *On the Priesthood* 6.1, 4. In one of his homilies on Acts, John also exclaims, "Teach me by your life, that is the best teaching!" *Hom. Acts*, NPNF¹ 11:192b.

19. See also 1 Cor. 4:16; Gal. 4:12; Phil. 3:17; 1 Thess. 1:6-7; 2 Thess. 3:6-13. See also Ignatius of Antioch, *Tralians* 7: "What is a bishop but someone who possesses great power and authority . . . , who according to his ability has been made an imitator of the Christ of God?"

20. Much like the classical virtue of prudence. *Duties of Leaders* 1.126 (XXVII).

21. See also *Didache* Ch. 15. Ambrose lists the following classical virtues in order of their importance for clergy: 1) prudence; 2) justice; 3) courage; 4) temperance (*Duties of Leaders* 1.115 [XXIV]), which he believes came from the Bible first (see Wis 8:7). See also Jerome, *Letter* LII, To Nepotian, NPNF² 6:95, and Gregory the Great, *Pastoral Rule* 2.1.

22. *Pastoral Rule* 2.1.

23. *Pastoral Rule* 1.3.

24. *Pastoral Rule* 2.6.

25. Sarah #5, in *Sayings of the Desert Fathers.*

26. *Pastoral Rule* 4.

27. *Christian Teaching* 1.22.20–40.44.

28. *On the Priesthood* 5.1-2.

29. *Pastoral Rule* 2.8; see also Ambrose, *Duties of Leaders* 2.29 (II.VII).

30. *Pastoral Rule* 2.8. On pleasing God alone, see also John Chrysostom, *On the Priesthood* 5.4-7.

31. *On the Priesthood* 3.9

32. *Homily on Acts*, NPNF¹ 11:192b.

33. Syncletica #26, in *Sayings of the Desert Fathers.*

34. Theodora #6, in *Sayings of the Desert Fathers.*

35. Augustine makes the observation in *Sermon* 340.2, commenting on 1 Tim. 3:6.

36. *Soliditas. Sermon* 339.1.

37. *Sermon* 340.1; see also *Sermon* 46.6-7.

38. *Pastoral Rule,* prefatory Letter to John, Fellow Bishop.

39. *Pastoral Rule* 2.3.

40. *Pastoral Rule* 4.

41. See also Jerome, *Letter* 52, To Nepotian, NPNF² 6:93.

42. *Letter* 14.9.

43. *On 1 Tim. 3:1.*

44. *Christian Teaching* 4.27.59–28.61.

45. The idea that the early church shifted from a charismatic form of leadership to an institutional one is a modern myth which is easily debunked by the evidence of church leadership throughout late antiquity. See most recently Claudia Rapp, *Holy Bishop in Late Antiquity: The Nature of Christian Leadership in an Age of Transition.* The Transformation of the Classical Heritage 37. Berkeley: University of California Press, 2005.

46. Theodora #5, in *Sayings of the Desert Fathers.*

47. *Didask. Apost.* 2.18: An unholy bishop is a positive threat to the community.

48. *Oration* 43.26.

49. *Pastoral Rule* 1.6.

50. *Oration* 2.15.

51. *Oration* 12.5. See also Theodore of Mopsuestia, *On 1 Tim.* 3:1.

52. See also 2 Cor. 6:7; 10:3-4; 13:1-4, 10.

53. *Letter* 13.

54. *De vita sua* 1649-1653.

55. *Sermon* 46.9.

56. *Exposition on Psalm.* 99:12.

57. Aug., *Ep* *18.3. See also *Sermon* 340a.8-10 and *Exposition on Psalm 132.4.*

58. *Sermon* 137.8-10.

59. *Exposition on Psalm* 64.10. See also *Sermon* 46.6-7.

60. Gregory Nazianzen thus alters the Platonic formula to say that only those who are *being* purified (not who are pure) can purify others. *Oration* 40.26. And he explicitly distances himself from the Novatianists: see *Oration* 33.16; 39.18-19.

III

1. *Oration* 2.16. Gregory Nazianzen may have borrowed the phrase from Origen's *Commentary on John* (13.303), where it refers to the body of Christian truth as a whole. Gregory the Great then took it from Gregory Nazianzen, ensuring its fame in Western circles: the care of souls is "the art of arts" (*Pastoral Rule* 1.1 [29]). Soon after Gregory Nazianzen, the phrase also appears in the Latin writer Macrobius (*Saturnalia* 7.15.14).

2. *Oration* 9.3.

3. *On the Priesthood* 4.2.

4. *On the Priesthood* 4.3.

5. *Carm.* 2.1.12.751-60.

6. Literally the "therapy of souls" (*therapeia psychon*). *Oration* 7.3.

7. Gregory the Great's *Pastoral Rule* is fuller only in the number of types of people and treatments that it recommends, which we will discuss below.

8. See Gregory Nazianzen, *Oration* 2.16.

9. In this sense, "soul" is not disconnected from "mind," as in certain anthropological schemes.

10. Parallel at Luke 12:4-7; see also Heb. 10:31.

11. Gregory Nazianzen, *Oration* 2.16, 26; 14.18, 37.

12. What Gregory calls "our habits, our passions, our lives, and our wills." *Oration* 2.18.

13. *Oration* 2.21.

14. *Pastoral Rule* 1.1.

15. *Oration* 2.20.

16. Syncletica #7, in *Sayings of the Desert Fathers*.

17. *Oration* 2.20-21.

18. *Oration* 2.10; 13.4.

19. *Oration* 2.16.

20. In addition to these biblical examples, Greek intellectual tradition had also long recognized the need to adapt one's words and deeds toward the situation and the particular needs of those one hopes to guide. See, e.g., Gorgias, *Pal.* 22; Plato, *Phdr.* 277.b-c. This method was developed further by Clement of Alexandria (see esp. *Strom.* 7) and later taken up most fully by Gregory Nazianzen and those who followed him, namely John Chrysostom and Gregory the Great.

21. *Oration* 2.28-29.

22. See Rom. 10:2.

23. *Oration* 2.39-42.

24. See also Eph. 4:13; Col. 2:19. Gregory Nazianzen, *Oration* 2.45. Here Gregory follows the teaching of Origen very closely; see, e.g., *On First Principles* 4; *On Prayer* 27.5-6; *Commentary on the Song of Songs,* prologue; *Against Celsus* 3.53.

25. See Matt. 15:18; also 12:34.

26. Gregory Nazianzen speaks of the "medicines" *(pharmakeiai)* that pastors administer: *Oration* 2.33.

27. *Oration* 2.30-32.

28. *Oration* 2.33.

29. *Pastoral Rule* 2.6.

30. *Pastoral Rule* 2.2. See also Gregory Nazianzen, *Oration* 27.3.

31. Gregory's Homeric observation (Odysseus was the "man of many turns") comes in *Oration* 2.16. For the musical comparison, see *Oration* 2.39; tamer of a monster: *Oration* 2.44.

32. *Sermon* 340.3.

33. *Pastoral Rule* 3.1.

34. *On Catechizing the Uninstructed* 5.9.

35. *On Catechizing the Uninstructed* 8.12.

36. *On Catechizing the Uninstructed* 9.13.

37. *Pastoral Rule* 1.11. For Gregory the Great, discernment *(discretio)* is crucial for good leadership, along with a contemplative knowledge of God.

38. Cassian, *Conf.* 2.2-4.

39. Cassian, *Conf.* 5.12.1.

40. *Rule of Saint Benedict* 2.

41. Cassian, *Conf.* 2.10-11.

42. *Exposition on Psalm* 103(2).11.

43. Cassian, *Conf.* 2.2, 16.

44. *Pastoral Rule* 2.6.

45. *Duties of Leaders* 2.120.

46. Cassian, *Conf.* 2.13.

47. *Oration* 2.44.

48. On pastoral adaptability, see also *Oration* 9.5-6; 13.4; 27.3-6; 37.1 (Jesus' own).

49. Jesus' rebukes of the Pharisees can be taken in a similar way. See also John 6:44.

50. *Duties of Leaders* 2.135.

51. *Duties of Leaders* 2.29.

52. *Duties of Leaders* 2.39.

53. *Duties of Leaders* 2.121-123.

54. Augustine, *haer.* 41.19.

55. See Cassian, *Inst.* book 4 on the gradual steps of monastic development.

56. *Conf.* 1.4.3.

57. *Pastoral Rule* 2.2.

58. *Oration* 2.52-56. See, in the order listed, Eph. 6:5-9; Rom. 8:1-3; Eph. 5:22, 25; 6:1-4; 1 Cor. 7; Rom. 14:3, 6; 1 Cor. 1:27; 3:18; Rom. 2:25, 29; Gal. 5:16; 1 Cor. 10:33.

59. *Oration* 2.29. Gregory's term here for pastoral management is *oikonomia*, "economy," the same used for God's overall relations with creation, and especially the saving work of Christ's incarnation.

60. *Oration* 2.21.

61. *Christian Teaching* 1.11.11.

62. *Christian Teaching* 1.11.12.

63. *Christian Teaching* 1.14.13.

64. *Christian Teaching* 1.11.11.

65. *On the Usefulness of Belief* 14.32.

66. *Christian Teaching* 2.5.6.

67. *Explanation of the Creed* 4; *On the Sacraments* 5.4.25.

IV

1. *Pastoral Rule* 1.1.

2. *Christian Teaching* 2.17.27–42.63.

3. *Oration* 2.23-26.

4. *Pastoral Rule*, Introductory Letter.

5. *Oration* 2.115.

6. *Christian Teaching* 3.5.

7. *Christian Teaching* 4.6-7.

8. *On Catechizing the Uninstructed* 6.10.

9. *Oration* 2.99.

10. E.g., *Carm.* 2.1.12.552-53; 608-9.

11. Gregory the Great, *Pastoral Rule* 2.11.

12. See *Against Heresies* 1.9.4.

13. Among the Pauline texts most influential on spiritual exegesis

(especially through Origen), see Rom. 7:14; 1 Cor. 2:10-16; 9:9-10; 10:11; 2 Cor. 3:6, 15-16; Gal. 4:24.

14. Or even confess that "Christ is Lord" in the first place (1 Cor. 12:3). See Origen, *First Principles* 1.3.4; *Cels.* 6.17.

15. *Comm. Jn.* 1.45.

16. See esp. *First Principles* pref; 1.1-3.

17. Origen's *First Principles,* Gregory's collected *Orations,* and Augustine's *Christian Teaching.*

18. *Christian Teaching* 4.5.7, trans. Hill adapt.

19. Origen, *First Principles* 4.1.1.

20. See also 1 Pet. 2:2: by feeding on "pure, spiritual milk," those who have rid themselves of evil will "grow into salvation."

21. *Oration* 2.96.

22. See also Prov. 1:7; Job 28:28.

23. *Christian Teaching* 2.7.11.

24. Or, "in the spirit, not the letter."

25. See also the "new Jerusalem" in Rev. 21:2. The theme originates in the prophets: see Ezek. 40; Zech. 2:6-9.

26. Paul is commenting on Deut. 25:4: "You shall not muzzle an ox while it is treading out the grain."

27. Origen, *Comm. Jn.* 1.24.

28. *Christian Teaching* prol.6-7 (with examples).

29. *First Principles* 4.2.9.

30. *Christian Teaching* 2.6.7.

31. *Christian Teaching* 3.1.

32. *Exposition on Psalm* 28.9.

33. Which Jews also practiced in late antiquity.

34. *Christian Teaching* 2.9.14. See also *Sermon* 46.35.

35. *Letter* 137.18.

36. *Christian Teaching* 1.11.11, 14.13, 17.16.

37. Augustine, *Letter* 105.14.

38. *Christian Teaching* 2.5.6.

39. See *Comm. Jn.* 13.23-42.

40. *First Principles* 4.3.14.

41. *First Principles* 1.8; 4.2.

42. *Christian Teaching* 2.7.10; *On Catechizing the Uninstructed* 4.8.

43. *Christian Teaching* 1.38.42.

44. *Oration* 2.99.

45. *Oration* 43.65.

46. *Oration* 22.12.
47. *Oration* 2.35-36.
48. *Christian Teaching* 1.5.5.
49. Gregory reads the syntax of this verse differently from modern interpreters; cf. the NRSV translation. The point of this passage would hold equally well in the modern reading.
50. *Oration* 31.3.
51. See Gregory, *Oration* 20.5; 28.31.
52. *Oration* 20.12.
53. *Oration* 21.8.
54. See *To Polycarp* 3; also *Didaskalia Apostolorum* 2.25.
55. *Oration* 42.4.
56. *Oration* 43.30, 33, 72.
57. *Carm.* 2.1.12.116-17.
58. *On the Priesthood* 4.3-4.
59. *Christian Teaching* prol.
60. See *Christian Teaching* 4.
61. *Duties of Leaders* 1.4.
62. *Duties of Leaders* 1.189.
63. *Letter* 52, To Nepotian, NPNF² 6:92.
64. *Pastoral Rule* 1.4.
65. *Pastoral Rule* 2.7.
66. *Pastoral Rule* 2.5.
67. *Pastoral Rule* 2.11.

V

1. *Oration* 2.35.
2. See Gregory Nazianzen, *Oration* 15.5; 14.12; Augustine, *inq. Jan.* 54.
3. *Oration* 25.2. See also Augustine, *Christian Teaching* 3.19.3.
4. *Christian Teaching* 3.19.3.
5. See Gregory Nazianzen, *Or.* 30.16.
6. *On the Priesthood* 3.5.
7. *Sermon* 296.1.
8. *Sermon* 95.1.
9. *Christian Teaching* 4.6.

10. Augustine, *On the Usefulness of Belief* 6.13; 7.17; see also *Letter* 95.6.

11. *Letter to Ammoun.*

12. *Letter to Draconitus* 2.

13. *Exposition on Psalm* 62.8.

14. *Exposition on Psalm* 71.5

15. *Oration* 1.6; see 2 Cor. 3:3.

16. *De vita sua* 1546-1549. "Thrones" refers to the bishop's seat in the cathedral and to the dignity of office. In this passage Gregory is being critical of those who use their high office to serve themselves rather than God's people.

17. *Oration* 3.7.

18. *Oration* 43.66.

19. *Sermon* 339.4.

20. *Sermon* 46.20.

21. *Pastoral Rule* 2.4.

22. *Pastoral Rule* 2.4.

23. *Christian Teaching* 4.2.3.

24. A concern for combating false teaching can be seen especially in Galatians, 1 and 2 Corinthians, Ephesians, Colossians, and 1 John.

25. Augustine, *Christian Teaching* 4.27, quoting Cicero, *The Orator* 21.69.

26. *Christian Teaching* 4.15.32; 17.34; 26.56.

27. *Christian Teaching* 4.4.6.

28. See *Christian Teaching* 4.12.28.

29. *Christian Teaching* 4.10.24.

30. *Christian Teaching* 4.10.25.

31. Gregory the Great, *Pastoral Rule* 3.39.

32. *Sermon* 46.2.

33. *Christian Teaching* 4.12.27.

34. *Christian Teaching* 4.61.

35. Gregory Nazianzen, *Oration* 43.48-50.

36. *Oration* 43.68.

37. *On the Priesthood* 4.4.

38. *On the Priesthood* 4.9.

39. *Christian Teaching* 4.12.28.

40. *Christian Teaching* 4.11.26.

41. *Christian Teaching* 4.10.25.

42. *Duties of Leaders* 1.101-2. See also Chrysostom, *On the Priesthood* 4.6-9.

43. *Christian Teaching* 28.61.

44. *Christian Teaching* 4.13.29.

45. See *Christian Teaching* 4.13.29.

46. *On the Priesthood* 2.3.

47. *Christian Teaching* 4.12.27. In this quotation I have altered the pronouns for the hearer from singular to plural.

48. *Christian Teaching* 4.24.53.

49. *Christian Teaching* 4.24.53.

50. *Christian Teaching* 4.4.6.

51. *On Catechizing the Uninstructed* 3.5-6.

52. *On Catechizing the Uninstructed* 4.8.

53. *Sermon* 387.1.

54. *Sermon* 46.10.

55. *Christian Teaching* 4.14.30-31.

56. *On Catechizing the Uninstructed* prol.2.3-4.

57. *Christian Teaching* 4.17.34f; 22.51.

58. *Christian Teaching* 4.22.51.

59. *Christian Teaching* 4.20.43.

60. *Christian Teaching* 4.28.61.

61. *Christian Teaching* 4.15.32; lit. "the piety of prayer"; see Matt. 10:19-20.

62. *Christian Teaching* 4.3.4-5.

63. *Christian Teaching* 4.5.7.

64. *Exposition on Psalm* 75.7.

65. See *Christian Teaching* 4.16.33.

66. *Exposition on Psalm* 118(32).4.

67. *Exposition on Psalm* 95.3.

68. *Exposition on Psalm* 67.15, 17.

69. *Christian Teaching* 4.27.59.

70. As Augustine tells Deogratias. *On Catechizing the Uninstructed* prol. 2.4.

71. *Exposition on Psalm* 56.17.

72. *Exposition on Psalm* 95.8.

73. *Exposition on Psalm* 103(1).11.

74. *Exposition on Psalm* 88.5-7.

75. *Exposition on Psalm* 103(2).11.

76. *Christian Teaching* 4.31.64.

77. *Sermon* 197.1.
78. Augustine, *Sermon* 387.2.
79. *Pastoral Rule,* Introductory Letter.
80. *Sermon* 5.1.
81. *Exposition on Psalm* 96.10, also quoted further in chapter one.
82. *Sermon* 216.1.

Acknowledgments

—ꟽꟽ—

I am grateful to the many people with whom I have had the privilege of discussing this material over the past several years: to my students at Berkeley and Yale Divinity Schools, the practicing church leaders who attended conferences and workshops, and an ecumenical group of colleagues who offered their comments at various stages of writing: Joseph Britton, Adela Yarbro Collins, Demetrios Katos, Bryan Spinks, and Thomas Troeger; and to my friends at the Episcopal Gathering of Leaders, especially Bishop Claude Payne, Mary MacGregor, and Belton Ziegler. My thanks are due as well to the Louisville Institute, which awarded me a Pastoral Leadership Grant that made the completion of this book possible, and to Yale Divinity School students Jamie Dunn and Andrew DeCarlow, who assisted me in my research and revisions.

Suggestions for Further Reading

—◊◊◊—

All of the translations are my own, except where noted. I have benefited from the published English translation, listed below, as well as others.

For those who wish to read more about the basic principles of pastoral ministry, the best thing to do will be to study the early sources directly. Further reading in modern sources can be found in the bibliographies in these volumes and in the standard reference works.

Gregory of Nazianzus, *Oration* 2 "On the Priesthood" is the earliest and most influential work on Christian pastoral ministry. Also illuminating are *Oration* 18 "On His Father," the funeral oration that Gregory delivered for his father, the former bishop of Nazianzus; and *Oration* 43 "On Basil the Great," a memorial oration for Gregory's late friend, the bishop of Caesarea. Each of these can be found in NPNF vol. II.7 (*Nicene and Post-Nicene Fathers,* edited by Philip Schaff. Peabody, Mass.: Hendrickson Publishers, 1994) and on several websites.

Ambrose of Milan, *On the Duties of the Clergy* (*De officiis* rendered here as *The Duties of Leaders*), translated by Rev. H. De

Romestrin. Oxford: Benediction Classics, 2010. For a more scholarly translation with facing Latin text, see *De officiis*, 2 volumes, edited with an introduction, translation, and commentary by Ivor J. Davidson. Oxford Early Christian Studies. Oxford: Oxford University Press, 2002.

Augustine of Hippo, *Teaching Christianity* (*De doctrina Christiana* rendered here as *Christian Teaching*), translated and edited by Edmund Hill, O.P. Works of St. Augustine 11. New York: New City Press, 1996. For a more scholarly edition, see *De Doctrina Christiana*, translated and edited by R. P. H. Green. Oxford Early Christian Studies. Oxford: Oxford University Press, 1996. Many of Augustine's sermons contain invaluable reflections on ordained ministry. Such passages can be found by consulting the indexes in the new translation contained in The Works of St. Augustine, Part III, volumes 1-2, translated by Edmund Hill, O.P. New York: New City Press, 1990-2009.

John Chrysostom, *Six Books on the Priesthood*, translated by Graham Neville. Popular Patristics Series. Crestwood, N.Y.: St. Vladimir's Seminary Press, 1996.

John Cassian, *Conferences*, translated and edited by Boniface Ramsey. Ancient Christian Writers 57. Mahwah, N.J.: Paulist Press, 1997. *Institutes*, translated by Boniface Ramsey. Ancient Christian Writers 58. Mahwah, N.J.: Paulist Press, 2000.

Gregory the Great, *The Book of Pastoral Rule*, translated by George E. Demacopoulos. Popular Patristic Series. Crestwood, N.Y.: St. Vladimir's Seminary Press, 2007.

Index of Names and Subjects

—ₘ—

Index of Scripture References

—ᴍ—